THE GREATEST COMPANY IN THE WORLD?

'During a time of global challenge and change, it is more vital than ever that the practice of businesses be underscored by a clear and thoughtful, environmentally responsible, person-centred ethic. Peter Casey's account of Tata provides a fascinating study of how a clear ethical code can ensure that business serves the needs of communities rather than communities serving the needs of business.'

—John Hume, recipient of the Nobel Peace Prize, the Gandhi Peace Prize and the Martin Luther King Peace Award

THE GREATEST COMPANY IN THE WORLD?

THE STORY OF TATA

PETER CASEY

ILLUSTRATIONS BY MIKE LUCKOVICH

PORTFOLIO
PENGUIN

PORTFOLIO
Published by the Penguin Group
Penguin Books India Pvt. Ltd, 7th Floor, Infinity Tower C, DLF Cyber City,
Gurgaon 122 002, Haryana, India
Penguin Group (USA) Inc., 375 Hudson Street, New York, New York 10014, USA
Penguin Group (Canada), 90 Eglinton Avenue East, Suite 700, Toronto, Ontario,
M4P 2Y3, Canada
Penguin Books Ltd, 80 Strand, London WC2R 0RL, England
Penguin Ireland, 25 St Stephen's Green, Dublin 2, Ireland (a division of
Penguin Books Ltd)
Penguin Group (Australia), 707 Collins Street, Melbourne, Victoria 3008, Australia
Penguin Group (NZ), 67 Apollo Drive, Rosedale, Auckland 0632, New Zealand
Penguin Books (South Africa) (Pty) Ltd, Block D, Rosebank Office Park,
181 Jan Smuts Avenue, Parktown North, Johannesburg 2193, South Africa

Penguin Books Ltd, Registered Offices: 80 Strand, London WC2R 0RL, England

First published in Portfolio by Penguin Books India 2014

Copyright © Peter Casey 2014

ISBN 9780670087686

For sale in the Indian Subcontinent only

Typeset in Sabon by R. Ajith Kumar, New Delhi
Printed at Replika Press Pvt. Ltd, India

A PENGUIN RANDOM HOUSE COMPANY

To Patsy and Leo Casey,
who taught me that there is no right way
to do the wrong thing

CONTENTS

CONTENTS

PREFACE

We are now living in a world where the richest eighty-five people own more than what 3.5 billion of the poorest own. This is a world, where, in 2013, the largest bank on the planet paid $23 billion in fines without admitting to any wrongdoing. The *Financial Times* reported that in 2013 the major banks in the United States paid over $100 billion in fines.

We are living in a world where, currently, 99 per cent of the wealth is owned by less than 1 per cent of the people, and if all the wealth in the world was divided into all the people in the world, everyone would be a millionaire.

I am an unapologetic capitalist, but I have now realized that there is a different way for capitalism to succeed—the Tata way.

Traditionally, companies are set up to make money for their shareholders, not to benefit the communities in which they exist and do business. Delivering return on investment is a necessity if you want to keep your job as a CEO of a publicly traded business. Serving the collective good, well, that's something for idealized socialist theory.

There has to be a better way, a new and better reality. There is. And this is the story about a truly unique company, which was established to create value for shareholders, employees, customers and humankind itself.

There simply is no other major business on earth like the Tata Group—a company whose bottom line every time is doing the right thing for society.

This company has not merely reformulated many of the business principles we have been taught for generations, it has turned them upside down.

Ask people who their heroes are, and you'll hear a lot of the same names. Mother Teresa, Martin Luther King Jr, Abraham Lincoln and Mahatma Gandhi will be popular choices. They were all phenomenal people—leaders, truly. But my own list is a little different.

My top three heroes—people who actually and positively changed the world we live in—are Leonardo da Vinci, Michelangelo Buonarroti and Jamsetji Tata.

The first two you've no doubt heard of. Leonardo da Vinci was, of course, one of the most creative geniuses the world has ever known. Michelangelo was widely regarded as the most talented and accomplished painter of his time, even earning the nickname 'the divine one'. Like Leonardo, Michelangelo changed the way we experience reality itself.

In my eyes, Jamsetji Tata, the founder of the Indian company that was to later become Tata Sons, is on a level with these undoubted luminaries, with a legacy that continues to change people's lives on a daily basis.

Few people—outside of India, at least—know the name Jamsetji Tata.

I certainly had never heard of him before 1999, when Gabriel Rozman announced to me that he was stepping down as director of Global Strategic Ventures and Acquisitions for accounting giant Ernst & Young. As

E&Y had long been a client of my executive recruiting firm, Claddagh Resources, I was curious as to where he was going.

'Tata,' he answered. The name barely rang a bell. But Gabriel enlightened me and, over the years, called on myself and Claddagh Resources to recruit top leaders for the India-based firm in France, Germany, Italy, Ireland, Netherlands, England, Canada and the United States. I was therefore in a position to get to know Tata Sons—there are more than 130 independently operating companies in the group—in a way few westerners ever do.

What I learned amazed me.

I decided to write this book initially to help my recruiters and executive search consultants have a better understanding of Tata Consultancy Services (TCS), who, over fourteen years, had become our biggest client.

It was supposed to just be a short fifteen-page summary, but the more I started studying TCS and Tata, the more captivated I got and the project developed a life of its own.

Now, there are amazing companies and amazing stories, but no amazing companies with amazing stories to match Tata's.

Today, Tata Group employs nearly half a million people, and earns revenues of $100 billion. It reported a profit of $6.23 billion in 2011–12, and controls assets valued at $77.7 billion.

Tata Sons was founded in 1868 by Jamsetji Tata, the son of the first businessman in what was otherwise a family of Zoroastrian Parsi priests. In 1869, Jamsetji converted a bankrupt oil mill for the production of cotton. It was a humble start, but Jamsetji Tata had grand visions—visions of what India, with his hard work, could become, visions worthy of the likes of Leonardo and Michelangelo.

Jamsetji knew and loved his religion, and he embraced its most central tenet: that the mission of the righteous person, the person who had hopes of heaven, was not merely to live a good life, but to make life better for others. He believed he could build a company that would spark positive change. While other successful capitalists and captains of industry started companies to create profit and, thereby, wealth, Jamsetji Tata planted the seeds of philanthropic trusts, which now own 66 per cent of the Tata Group. In harmony with his religion, Tata's company would exist—ultimately—to finance and initiate projects to improve the lives of the people of India.

So, Jamsetji Tata became not only a catalyst for sweeping change in his vast homeland, but, in the process, conceptualized an entirely new way of doing business as well as philanthropy. What he began has changed the lives of billions, as the company he founded continues to work for the betterment of society. In the words of Jamsetji: 'We think we started on sound and straightforward business principles, considering the interests of the shareholders our own, and the health and welfare of the employees, the sure foundation of our success.'[1]

This book will introduce you to my hero—and to the legacy that is his creation. My hope for the book is that it will encourage companies and governments—

---

[1] 'The quotable Jamsetji Tata', March 2008; available online at: http://www.tata.com/aboutus/articlesinside/1U2QamAhqtA=/ TLYVr3YPkMU=.

encourage *you*—to emulate and implement the Tata model. I know the world would be a better place if that were to happen.

Tata by the Numbers

1. Two-thirds of Tata is owned by philanthropic trusts. Tata is one of the biggest charities in the world.

2. Tata consists of more than 130 companies, of which thirty-two are traded on stock exchanges.

3. Two of the top twenty companies in India in terms of market capitalization—TCS and Tata Motors—are members of the Tata Group.

4. Tetley, a Tata company, is the second-largest tea producer in the world.

5. The largest company in India (as measured by market capitalization), TCS, is the largest member of the group.

6. Tata is the biggest industrial-sector employer in the United Kingdom. This is a huge achievement for a company from a former colony of the realm.

7. Tata revenues exceed $100 billion.

8. Tata Steel is the fifth-largest steel company in the world.

9. Tata Power is India's largest private-sector power provider—and 13 per cent of their electricity is generated by clean sources such as hydro, solar and wind.

This economic powerhouse is two-thirds owned by philanthropic trusts. It is, in effect, a profitable charity. However, there is no need to argue theories of capitalism and altruism. A glance at the group's P & L reveals that Tata is highly successful—and has been for some 140 years.

So, how does a highly diversified conglomerate become a charity or vice versa? How does a philanthropic for-profit satisfy its stakeholders?

The Fourth Stakeholder

While many of its companies are publicly traded, the Tata Group has evolved from being a family-owned business to becoming one of the best-run, professionally managed groups in the world. The philanthropic trusts control a majority of the Tata holding company, Tata Sons. The Tata family is a very small shareholder. Yet, the owners are only one of four stakeholders Tata sets out to serve. In addition to the owners (which includes shareholders) are employees, customers and society itself.

Society is what the company's leaders call the Fourth Stakeholder. And it looms large, maybe the largest, among all four.

Society drove Jamsetji Tata when he built his first company more than a century ago. He did not use so abstract or neutral a term, however, but undertook his enterprise with the active mission of using it simply to make people's lives better.

Even in our cynical age, we cannot fail to recognize such nobility of purpose and principle. But if we are tempted to ascribe such nobility to a bygone era, the fact is that Tata Sons unvaryingly adheres to the principle on which it was founded. Even through financial crises, it has not wavered.

The spectacle of an enterprise as highly moral as it is profitable is rare in a society which has grown accustomed to thinking of business success as a zero-sum game, in which my triumph requires your defeat.

Success that follows a zero-sum formula is incompatible with a Fourth Stakeholder. But Jamsetji Tata and those who followed him never used that formula. They reformulated the criteria of business success, and made humanity, philanthropy and ethics not adjuncts to profit but its very core. And, so, whether measured in dollars, rupees, euros or service to humankind, Tata has certainly become a role model of success.

Tata companies continually aspire to better ethics, just as they are committed to better business practices. The two are not only quite compatible, they are essential to one another. The company has not merely reformulated many of the business principles we have been taught for generations, it has turned them upside down. Most significantly, Tata management long ago rejected the dictum that a shoemaker should stick to his last. Instead of specializing, Tata has ventured into an array of unrelated industries and has become a world leader in several—from steel and chemicals to IT consulting, hotels, aviation, energy, education, automobile manufacturing and insurance.

These are just a few of the Tata arms. In fact, it is easier to think of an industry that Tata is *not* involved in than to list those that they are. A diversified global enterprise, philanthropic at its core, the company shares profits with employees, shareholders and the societies in which they live and work. The most senior Tata managers don't live in multiple sprawling mansions, as so many American and European CEOs do, but in modest apartments and homes.

The guiding principle for everyone at Tata is sharing the wealth. With Tata reporting annual profits in 2012 of $6.23 billion, this means that a very large amount of money is invested back into the economy every year just from this one source.

PART I

THE TATA STORY

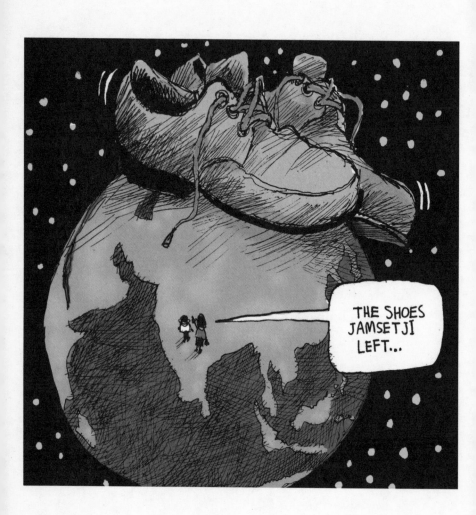

ONE

JAMSETJI TATA STARTS A NEW BUSINESS

Jamsetji Tata (1839–1904) was a man of business, who saw companies as tools for building profound, positive and lasting change. He founded a company not merely to make profit and create personal wealth, but to improve the lives of his fellow Indians. That is where the Tata story starts.

The first prime minister of India, Jawaharlal Nehru, memorialized Jamsetji Tata as 'one of the big founders of modern India'. He was, Nehru said, a man who took 'the lead in action, in ideas', a lead that did not 'fit in with the very climate of opinion', and a lead, therefore,

3

that showed 'true courage . . . and vision'. The prime minister echoed others in calling Jamsetji a 'visionary' and a 'nation builder'. Nehru would doubtless have also agreed with the many who called Jamsetji 'the father of Indian industry'.[1]

By all accounts, the soft-spoken Jamsetji was passionate, warm, humble and driven. These qualities seem to have been encoded in the DNA he passed down to his sons and successors as well. The mission of the multi-billion-dollar Tata companies remains as vividly true today as it was more than a hundred years ago, when Jamsetji embarked on his first modest entrepreneurial venture.

If Jamsetji reformulated what it means to be a captain of industry, he also redefined the role of philanthropist. Westerners have sometimes compared him to Andrew Carnegie, who occupies a prominent space in the pantheon of nineteenth- and early-twentieth-century industrialists-turned-philanthropists which also includes the likes of J.P. Morgan and John D. Rockefeller.

---

[1] 'The quotable Jamsetji Tata', March 2008; available online at: http://www.tata.com/aboutus/articlesinside/1U2QamAhqtA=/TLYVr3YPkMU=.

The difference between these men and Jamsetji Tata is that the Americans built and ran their businesses first, for profit, and only then, after they had made their millions, did they begin thinking about how to share that wealth. Their contributions were—and their endowments continue to be—profoundly important, but they do not erase a history of careers in dog-eat-dog capitalism. Carnegie the philanthropist was also Carnegie the ruthless strike-breaker. Morgan the art collector was also Morgan the monopolist. Rockefeller the endower of medical research and so much else was also the Rockefeller whose Standard Oil Trust made him the most hated and feared figure in American business.

Jamsetji, in contrast, reflexively thought about others first. The company he built was built for the express purpose of helping the less fortunate and improving everyone's lives, including those of his workers. As great as the philanthropy of Carnegie, Morgan and Rockefeller was, it was an afterthought. But for Jamsetji Tata, it was the driving thought.

Son of an Entrepreneur, Grandson of Priests

Jamsetji was the only son of the five children born to Nusserwanji and Jeevanbai Tata. He was born on 3 March 1839 in Navsari, one of the oldest cities in Gujarat, the Indian state known as the Jewel of the West. Navsari was already more than a thousand years old in the twelfth century, when members of the Zoroastrian Parsi religion settled there, making it a centre of religious culture and learning.

Nusserwanji Tata's father was one in a very long line of Parsi priests and was the first Tata to break with tradition by deciding to become an entrepreneur and banker instead of a holy man. Yet, Nusserwanji by no means broke with his religion, the values of which he passed down to Jamsetji, who further passed it down to his two sons. Chief among these values was the mission to lift others from suffering and improve their lives. In this way, a person becomes righteous and worthy of heaven.

Still, like his father, Jamsetji embarked on a business career. In 1853, at fourteen, he joined his father in Bombay (now Mumbai). He enrolled in Elphinstone

College, from which he graduated in 1858, having married Hirabai Daboo while he was still a student. The couple would have two sons, Dorabji and Ratanji, future Tata Company leaders.

Upon graduating, Jamsetji joined his father's trading business and quickly came to understand the intricacies of commodities trading, markets and banking. His Elphinstone education had been no ivory-tower experience. He had lived through the turbulence of the Indian Rebellion of 1857, and subsequent travel through continental Europe, England and America broadened his education and opened his eyes to what he perceived as vast opportunities available to Indian business.

He also had a first-hand education in business failure with the collapse of his father's trading company. His travels in England could not have been much fun, as he had to endure the complaints of local businessmen, some of whom had suffered major losses thanks to his father. Clearly, the experience did not discourage Jamsetji Tata. Not only did he found his own trading company in 1868 at the age of twenty-nine, but his English sojourn may have deeply planted in his conscience an overriding need to 'make things right' with his own customers many years later.

In 1869, a year after founding his first company, Jamsetji started another. His travels in England had included close-up tours of the country's many new textile mills. Applying this experience, Jamsetji bought a bankrupt oil mill in Chinchpokli, located, at the time, on the outskirts of Bombay. He converted it to cotton production, named it Alexandra Mill, and achieved a success sufficient to attract a buyer two years later. He resolved to sink the profit from this sale into a new venture.

Uncommon Sense

After the sale, Jamsetji decided to continue in the cotton industry. That certainly made sense—but what seemed to violate common sense was his decision to look far beyond Bombay and its environs to set up his new mill. What businessman would deliberately turn his back on the bustling Indian city? A businessman of uncommon sense. A man who—to borrow the phrase Steve Jobs coined for Apple—dared to think different.

Jamsetji travelled more than 800 kilometres inland from Bombay to Nagpur, in central India, a location in the heart of cotton country, though remote from almost everything else. Indeed, compared to Bombay, it was deserted. Jamsetji, however, saw it as a clean slate when he opened the Central India Spinning, Weaving and Manufacturing Company on 1 January 1877. Since the mill commenced operations on the same day that Queen Victoria was installed as empress of India, Jamsetji named the establishment Empress Mills.

By the time of the name change, Jamsetji's cotton enterprise was highly successful. But, already, he had visions of something far larger—for his company and his country. He would build his business to be bigger and better—big enough and good enough to make a difference in the life of India. 'In a free enterprise,' he would say later, 'the community is not just another stakeholder in business, but is in fact the very purpose of its existence.'[2] The combination of his world travels, his Parsi religious heritage and the profound sense of

---

[2] Ann Graham, 'Too Good to Fail', *Strategy + Business*, 23 February 2010, Spring 2010 / Issue 58. Available online at: http://www.strategy-business.com/article/10106?pg=all.

responsibility that success had brought him led Jamsetji Tata to set three goals for his business life.

The First Goal: Build an Iron and Steel Plant

Around 1880, while he was visiting Manchester, in the heart of industrial England, researching new machinery for Empress Mills, Jamsetji attended a lecture by the celebrated philosopher, essayist and social critic Thomas Carlyle. 'Those who control the iron and steel will in time come to control the gold as well,' Carlyle remarked to his Manchester audience. And Jamsetji had an epiphany.

In a single sentence, Carlyle had outlined a formula for change on a very large scale. It inspired in Jamsetji a vision of an iron and steel company capable of bringing gold to India, transforming the country, lifting at least some of its crushing poverty and making the growth of truly metropolitan cities possible. With iron and steel, the construction of great buildings, including those of heavy industry, could elevate India from its backward agricultural existence to a place among the great industrial powers of the world.

Most entrepreneurs think big. That's what they do. But Jamsetji thought bigger. He envisioned not just a steel mill, but one of such scale and excellence that it would be the envy of the entire world. Yet, he soon discovered that, among prominent Indians, he was almost alone in his vision. The vast majority saw no need for such a facility. Moreover, as few as there were who appreciated the value of a state-of-the-art steel mill, far fewer thought that building and running such a plant in India was even possible. Jamsetji sought encouragement from the chief commissioner of the Great Indian Peninsula Railway, only to be rebuffed. The chief swore to 'eat every pound of steel rail the Tatas succeed in making'.[3]

Instead of being discouraged by the commissioner's oath, Jamsetji took it as a challenge. He hired the best American geologist he could find to locate suitable iron ore in India. When that failed to produce results, Jamsetji and his sons devoted years in an effort to pinpoint the iron fields. In the end, it was the discovery

---

[3] Nirmalya Kumar, *India's Global Powerhouses: How They Are Taking On the World* (Boston: Harvard Business Review Press, 2009), p. 160.

11

of iron-ore deposits in the hills of Gorumahisani in the state of Mayurbhanj by an Indian geologist Pramatha Nath Bose that proved the key. Following the discovery, Bose wrote a letter to Jamsetji Tata on 24 February 1904, which led to the establishment of the Tata Iron and Steel Company. The next challenge was to engineer water delivery, but once that was solved, construction of the plant began at the village of Sakchi, now in the state of Jharkhand.

Even before ground was broken, Jamsetji was thinking in ways quite foreign to the builders of the nineteenth-century Industrial Revolution. His tours of England's industrial towns had shown him exactly what he did *not* want for his steelworkers. The English mill towns like Liverpool and Manchester offered workers filthy slums. The belts of England had industrialized so rapidly that builders accommodated the sudden surge of workers by carving out terraced housing on barren hillsides, using the cheapest materials available, and depending mostly on gravity to handle sewage. The result created conditions that made dysentery, typhus and typhoid endemic.

Jamsetji resolved not to make the same mistakes. He committed himself to a different path for India. He began by taking the costly and unconventional step of hiring a town planner. In addition to installing a water-filtration system to avoid water pollution, he built dedicated outhouses and a grain depot—both unknown in the English mill towns. He wanted to attract and maintain a cadre of skilled workers in his new town, and so he made himself responsible for promoting their well-being. It was a wise human resources investment, of course, but his concern was also the product of a deep sense of responsibility, and was the very essence of the ethos of the servant-leader—one who cares for others, so that they can better care for themselves, and perform, with excellence, the work that is expected of them.

At this point in the Industrial Revolution, managers thought nothing of exploiting their employees. Jamsetji took a different approach. He felt that it was his duty not just to make living conditions tolerable, but to actually improve his workers' lives. His companies offered shorter working hours; provided more comfortable working conditions, with special attention to adequate ventilation (perceived as a 'luxury' at the beginning of the twentieth century); and created both a pension fund at Empress Mills (1886 Provident Fund) and an accident fund (1895 Accident Compensation Fund) at a time when these were rare in the West and almost unheard of in the East.

In 1902, Jamsetji began drawing up elaborate plans for creating a truly modern industrial town. His objective was to provide a quality of life his employees would enjoy. Even before the final site had been identified, he devoted a great deal of time to describing the environment he wanted. His requirements included 'wide streets planted with shady trees, every other of the quick-growing variety'.[4] He called for plenty of space for lawns and gardens as well as large areas for football and hockey fields and parks. To ensure that all who came to work for him could continue to practise their diverse faiths within the community, he incorporated 'Hindu temples, Islamic mosques, and Christian churches'.

In short, Jamsetji was a visionary who recognized the

---

[4] 'The quotable Jamsetji Tata', March 2008; available online at: http://www.tata.com/aboutus/articlesinside/1U2QamAhqtA=/TLYVr3YPkMU=.

importance of building a social community to support the industrial community. He believed that Tata Steel would fail unless he created a desirable community to attract the best and brightest workers. The result was the transformation of Sakchi into an enduring model for urban planning and community. In 1919, Lord Chelmsford renamed the city Jamshedpur in honour of Jamsetji Tata, whose birthday is celebrated there as Founder's Day.

Jamsetji Tata would not live to see his steel mill or his city completed. On 19 May 1904, while travelling in Germany on business, the sixty-five-year-old business titan succumbed to an illness. Dorab Tata oversaw the completion of construction, and on 25 August 1907, the Tata Iron and Steel Company was formally founded. The first steel ingot was produced in 1912 under the supervision of Dorab and his cousin R.D. Tata. Neither held the doubting chief commissioner to his oath—that he would eat all the first steel the Tatas managed to produce. Good thing, too. By 1939, Tata was operating the biggest steel mill in the British Empire, and today, with manufacturing operations in twenty-six countries, Tata Steel is the fifth-largest steel maker on the planet.

PETER CASEY

The Second Goal: Hydroelectric Power for India

As Jamsetji would not live to see his steel plant, he would die before his company realized his second goal—the construction of a vast hydroelectric plant. In the early twentieth century, Indian factories and mills relied exclusively on coal for energy. As a result of his world travels, Jamsetji saw that there was a better source—hydroelectric power. Jamsetji not only recognized the importance of low-cost energy to India's continued growth and expansion on a global scale, but it was clear to him that replacing coal with water-produced electricity would greatly reduce the smog and soot that suffocated Bombay and other Indian cities. A visit to Niagara Falls, in particular, seared into his brain an image of the awesome power of water. He understood that his first step would be to find a water source on which he could build a power plant. But where would he find a waterfall anywhere near Bombay?

One day, it came to him.

After monsoonal rains in Bombay, Jamsetji hired a boat for a cruise of Bombay Harbour, intending to show

16

his top executives the magnitude of the water flowing into the harbour from the Roha river.

'All this water from the Western Ghats is wasted,' he told his managers. 'We should harness it to produce hydroelectric power.'[5] Seeing the demonstration of power for themselves, they agreed, and the project was authorized. The Tata Hydro-Electric Power Supply Company was established in 1910. Today, Tata Power is India's largest private electric company, providing 4 per cent of the nation's electric power.

The Third Goal: A World-Class Science Institute in India

Jamsetji Tata's central belief was that the key resource that India must leverage to lift itself out of poverty was the raw talent and skills of its people. This, he knew, would not happen by itself. What India needed were world-class educational institutions. And so his third

---

[5] Reeba Zachariah, 'Tata Power forms equal JV with Norway's SN', *The Economic Times*, 2 November 2009; available online at: http://articles.economictimes.indiatimes.com/2009-11-02/news/28441349_1_tata-power-bhira-hydropower-business.

life goal became the establishment of a science institute. Accordingly, in 1898, Jamsetji donated fourteen buildings and four other properties in Bombay for the establishment of a university dedicated to science. The gift was spectacular, representing approximately half his fortune, about 10 million rupees—roughly $4.56 million in 1898—which is equivalent to $140 million today.

The idea of creating a science university met with enthusiasm and widespread agreement, yet progress on creating the institution moved slowly. It would be a dozen years before the Indian Institute of Science opened its doors, in Bangalore, in 1911—seven years after Jamsetji's death.

The institute was not, however, his first foray into education. As early as 1892, Jamsetji had endowed a scholarship fund to enable deserving Indian students to obtain an education abroad at some of the world's great research universities. It was all too clear to him that Indian universities were not committed to study and innovation, and rather than waste valuable time—and human resources—in what would surely be a prolonged effort to create change in Indian higher education,

Jamsetji looked to the outside world. By 1924, it was estimated that some 20 per cent of all Indian Civil Service employees had been beneficiaries of the Tata endowment.

Still, during his lifetime, Jamsetji never abandoned his conviction that improving the Indian system of education was critical to the country's strength and development. In his later years, education—Indian education—became the central focus of his life. He envisioned a university curriculum that included the study of science and technology, medicine and sanitation (including bacteriology), philosophy and education, ethics and psychology, Indian history and archaeology, and statistics and economics. The depth and breadth of courses would position the new university to be the best in the country—and among the best in the world. When he donated half his fortune to the project, Jamsetji drew the attention of the entire nation. Not that everyone saw the wisdom of his gesture. Some thought he was a fool for throwing his money away. What jobs would graduates have available to them in India, they asked. Indeed, at the time, there were few answers. Amid many doubters and doubts, the approval of the new institute came slowly—not until 1909, five years after Jamsetji's death.

The Taj Mahal Hotel

Jamsetji's grandest initiatives took many years to come to fruition; his three biggest dreams were achieved after his death. One highly ambitious dream did come true before his passing, however. It was the product of a vision for a luxury hotel in Bombay. According to some, the source of this passion was Jamsetji's having been denied entry to a grand Bombay hotel because he was an Indian. But this, almost certainly, never actually happened. The truth is that Jamsetji Tata built the Taj Mahal Hotel because the so-called luxury hotels in Bombay at the time were, in fact, little more than hovels. In them, the rats were as plentiful as the menus were limited. Few Americans or Europeans could be enticed to stay in them.

Without a truly luxurious hotel, built and run in accordance with world-class standards, Bombay—the biggest city in India—would never be a world-class destination. Jamsetji envisioned an opulent hotel as a great and valuable gift he could give the city. In love with the very idea, he funded its construction personally. As usual, sceptics questioned the need. Then they questioned the suitability of an Indian to build it. Once again, Jamsetji persevered against all opposition. He invested an estimated 42 million rupees (the equivalent of $176 million today) to bring his idea to life. When it opened in 1903, the scoffers were forgotten. The hotel quickly became the pride of India.

Although 'eating houses' or restaurants were common in Bombay at the time, fine dining and luxury accommodation were not. The Taj was among the most elegant hotels in the world. It was, in fact, the first building in Bombay to have electricity, and its use of American electric fans, German-made elevators, Turkish baths and English butlers represented the cutting edge of innovation in hotel amenities. The Taj also featured the city's first-ever licensed bar, the first restaurant serving meals all day, and the country's very first nightclub.

Furthering His Vision

On his deathbed, Jamsetji Tata implored his family to

continue all that he had begun. 'If you cannot make it greater, at least preserve it. Do not let things slide. Go on doing my work and increasing it, but if you cannot, do not lose what we have done.'[6] He asked this not for selfish reasons—not because he wanted to claim credit—but because he knew how important all the products of his vision were to the future of India.

Jamsetji Tata: Themes of a Career

The story of Jamsetji Tata is more than the sum of a life's chronology. Every key element of the man's make-up has figured as an abiding theme in the history of the Tata Group and its major companies.

Jamsetji's commitment to philanthropy, his dedication to serving the needs of others and to improving the lives of all, his intense Indian patriotism, his innovative approach to practically everything, his refusal to compromise on ethics, his commitment to public transparency, his embrace of independence within

---

[6] 'The quotable Jamsetji Tata', March 2008; available online at: http://www.tata.com/aboutus/articlesinside/1U2QamAhqtA=/TLYVr3YPkMU=.

a core corporate community, his passion for setting massive goals and doing great things, his aim to create evolutionary and enduring transformation, and his style of servant leadership—each of these, through time, has continued as a theme in the narrative of the company he founded.

SIR DORABJI TATA

TWO

SIR DORABJI TATA

In many ways, Dorabji is the unsung hero of Tata—a sportsman, statesman and far-sighted leader, who gifted India both the Olympic ideal and a trust foundation that brought hope to many over the years.

Dorabji (or Dorab, as he was generally called) took over as chairman of the Tata Group of companies after his father's passing in 1904. Although Jamsetji has been generally hailed as the visionary, and his son as the man who essentially took his late father's plans through execution, Dorab was much more than a mere lieutenant. He was himself a leader and a true visionary, who took his father's plans and goals and not only brought them to fruition, but, along with his brother Ratan Tata, improved them greatly.

Following in His Father's Footsteps

The eldest son of Jamsetji and Hirabai Tata, Dorab was born in 1859 and grew up primarily in Bombay. He attended proprietary high school and was then sent to England to continue his education with a private tutor. In 1877, he enrolled at Gonville and Caius College, Cambridge. It was here that the eighteen-year-old's love of sports emerged. He won awards in cricket and football and distinguished himself in rowing, running and riding. After two years, he returned to India at his grandfather's request to enrol at St Xavier's College.

After graduating, Dorab became a journalist with the *Bombay Gazette*, but soon fell under the spell of his family's business. In 1884, he left the paper to join Tata's cotton division at Empress Mills, where one of his earliest assignments was to travel to Mysore to explore opportunities for expansion there. Once the viability of growth there was confirmed, Dorab obtained the necessary government approvals with impressive speed.

Jamsetji was eager for his son to meet the highly regarded Dr H.J. Bhabha while he was in Mysore. During their first meeting, Dorab also met Bhabha's young daughter Meherbai, and it is said that he fell in love with her at first sight. The two were married in 1897, when Dorab was thirty-eight and Meherbai just eighteen. The union was a happy one, although the couple had no children.

A Dream Materialized

Back in Bombay, Dorab took the challenge of supporting his father's vision to heart. Working under Jamsetji and then assuming the chairman role upon his father's death in 1904, Dorab laboured tirelessly towards creating a modern iron and steel industry in India. Tata Steel and Tata Power now exist because of Dorab's perseverance and personal involvement in their creation. In addition to founding new companies, Dorab also fostered expansion across the group. He helped to establish three hydroelectric power companies, an oil and soap company, an insurance business and two cement companies, in addition to supporting J.R.D. Tata's aviation unit and investing in the progress of science and medicine through the establishment of the Indian Institute of Science.

He was knighted in the New Year's Honours List in 1910—a recognition of the devotion and courage with which, in furthering his father's projects, he had also served the country. Not that Dorab's tenure as chairman was without critical challenges. Dorab used the post-World War I economic expansion to propel the exponential growth of Tata. This went remarkably well until 1924, when a perfect storm of economic events collided with progress. That year, prices skyrocketed in response to transportation and labour issues in the West. With rising costs came precipitous declines in revenue. On top of this, a massive earthquake that suddenly drove down demand for pig iron hit Tata Steel's largest customer, Japan.

Dorab may not have realized just how bad things were until he received a telegram from Jamshedpur announcing that Tata Steel did not have enough money on hand to pay its employees. Unable to pay wages from corporate funds, Dorab pledged his own wealth and his wife's jewels to qualify for a bank loan, which would allow the company to continue operating. This personal risk-taking proved critical to the survival of Tata Steel. And when revenue began to rise thanks to expanded production, the loan was repaid.

A Passion for Sport

Dorab's passion for sport led him to advocate India's participation in the Olympics as early as 1919, much before the nation had established its own Olympic committee.

He explained his motivation thus:

Having been educated in my youth in England, I had shared in nearly every kind of English athletics and acquired a great love for them. On my return to India I conceived the idea of introducing a love for such things there. I helped set up, with the support of English friends, a High School Athletic Association amongst numerous schools of Bombay, in the first place for cricket and then for athletics meetings, which embraced nearly all the events which form part of the Inter-University contests every year in London.[1]

For Dorab, adopting a game also meant adopting European clothes, rules and notions of order and 'fair play'. Sport became the playing field where tradition and modernity met, clashed and fused.

He was elected president of the Deccan Gymkhana, an athletics meeting which took place in Pune. The Gymkhana committee wanted to develop their sports programme more in line with established Indian traditions, but Dorab insisted on fusing the two cultures.

Dorab found that the competitors were 'all boys of the peasant class working in the fields and living off poor fare'[2], with the organizers proposing to run their 100-yard heats around a bend, without strings, because their sports ground was very small and the track was part of a rough unrolled grass field.

---

[1] Boria Majumdar and Nalin Mehta, *India and the Olympics* (New York: Routledge, 2009), p. 9.
[2] 'Tata's Olympic safari', *Times of India*, 3 August 2008; available online at: http://timesofindia.indiatimes.com/home/stoi/deep-focus/ tatas-olympic-safari/articleshow/3319673.cms.

Other popular events included a long-distance race of over 25 miles, rightly designated as the marathon. The peasants who participated were used to running barefoot on hard, macadamized or dirt roads. Despite their lack of training and the primitive conditions, the first three or four men ran the distance in fair time. As Dorab observed, their time 'would compare well with the times done in Europe or elsewhere'.[3] In 1919, some of their performances were close to the times clocked in the Olympics.

With hope in his heart, Dorab decided to send three of the runners, at his own expense, to the Antwerp Games of 1920. 'I hoped that with proper training and food under English trainers and coaches they might do credit to India. This proposal fired the ambition of the nationalist element in that city to try and send a complete Olympic team,' he later explained in a letter to the International Olympic Committee president, Count Baillet Latour, in 1929.

The peasant athletes had little idea of what was

---

[3] Boria Majumdar and Nalin Mehta, *India and the Olympics* (New York: Routledge, 2009), p. 10.

required to participate in the Olympics or of the standard of performance essential to qualify for any of the events. For instance, a key member of the Gymkhana, when asked what time he thought was standard for a 100-yard race, replied that it could be anything 'from half a minute to a minute'. He was astounded when told that it was not a matter of minutes but rather of tenths of seconds.

Dorab became president of the fledgling Indian Olympic Council and personally financed the Indian team's participation in the 1924 Games in Paris—where it is reported that his wife, Meherbai Tata, took part in the tennis mixed doubles fixtures. Meherbai was a top tennis player and had won many national level tournaments in the early 1920s.

Dorab saw the value of India having its own team at the Olympics, while it was still under British rule. It was not just a matter of pride, it was an early step towards independence.

He regularly scouted for sporting talent and established training clubs and facilities to develop it. The Willingdon Sports Club, the Parsi Gymkhana, the High

Schools Athletic Association and the Bombay Presidency Olympic Games Association were all initiated by Dorab. Thanks to his involvement, India won the gold medal in hockey at the 1928 Olympics in Amsterdam.

Reinvesting in India

In 1932, nearing the end of his life, and following the loss of his wife to leukaemia, Dorab placed his entire fortune of over 10 million rupees (the equivalent of $64 million in today's times) in trust, to be used 'without any distinction of place, nationality or creed, for the advancement of learning and research, the relief of distress, and other charitable purposes'.[4]

In establishing the Sir Dorab Tata Trust, he said:

To my father, the acquisition of wealth was only a secondary object in life; it was always subordinate to the constant desire in his heart to improve the industrial and intellectual condition of the people of

---

[4] 'In the name of the father'; available online at: http://www.tata. co.in/aboutus/articlesinside/!$$$!vi!$$$!KywJPS4=/TLYVr3YP- kMU=.

this country; and the various enterprises which he from time to time undertook in his lifetime had, for their principal object, the advancement of India in these important respects. Kind fate has, however, permitted me to help in bringing to completion his inestimable legacy of service to the country, and it is a matter of the greatest gratification to his sons to have been permitted to carry to fruition the sacred trust which he committed to their charge.[5]

Soon after this, in April of the same year, as a memorial to his wife, he endowed the Lady Tata Memorial Trust with a corpus of 2.5 million rupees (the equivalent of $16 million in today's times) for research into leukaemia. The Lady Meherbai D. Tata Education Trust was formed as a much smaller trust, partly from public donations, for the training of women in hygiene, health and social welfare.

---

[5] 'Dorabji Tata while laying the foundation stone of the Lonavala Dam, 8th February 1911'; available online at: http://www.tatasteel.com/investors/annual-report-2010-11/html/hd3.html.

The First Three Tata Trusts

- The Sir Dorabji Tata Trust supports the Tata Institute of Social Sciences, the Tata Memorial Centre for Cancer Research and Treatment, the Tata Institute of Fundamental Research, the National Centre for the Performing Arts, the National Institute of Advanced Studies, and the Sir Dorabji Tata Centre for Research in Tropical Diseases.

- The Lady Tata Memorial Trust funds research into leukaemia.

- The Lady Meherbai D. Tata Education Trust supports advanced education for women.

Dorabji died of a heart attack on 3 June 1932, leaving behind a stronger Tata and India, on and off the field.

THREE

SIR NOWROJI SAKLATWALA

The son of Jamsetji's sister, Nowroji Saklatwala, became the third chairman of the Tata Group after the death of his cousin Sir Dorabji Tata in 1932. He was immediately confronted with the unenviable task of consolidating the company during the global depression of the 1930s. His upbringing and his fascination with the game of cricket gave him the skills to carry the company through this difficult period in a six-year reign that was to see Tata take great social as well as economic strides.

Born in 1875 to Bapuji and Virbaiji Saklatwala, Nowroji, like his first cousin Dorabji, attended St Xavier's College in Bombay. He began his working life as an apprentice in one of the Tata mills, earning a starting salary of 50 rupees a month.

Nowroji was a quick learner, impressing those around him with his work ethic and ability to understand the intricacies of both the cotton products being created and the economics of the industry. His keen intellect saw him promoted to lead the mills department within a few short years.

Even after a long day of working in the mills, Nowroji rarely turned down an invitation to play a game of cricket. In addition to keeping him fit, the game honed him in the important leadership skills of working collaboratively, maintaining morale and compromising when needed.

As his professional star continued to rise within Tata, so did his reputation on the cricket field. Nowroji played first-class cricket for the Parsi team of 1904–05, representing them against the Europeans. However, his workload at Tata soon prevented him from continuing to play as a team member.

In 1917, Nowroji was named chairman of the Bombay Mill-Owners' Association—a sign of the trust and respect the industry had for him. Four years later, he represented Indian employers at the International Labour Conference in Geneva. Nowroji served his industry in many ways, including working as an honorary adviser on virtually any committee that asked him for counsel. His energy and devotion to his work knew no bounds.

During World War I, he was associated with many committees and rendered particularly meritorious service as honorary adviser to the Munitions Board during 1919–21.

Within Tata, Nowroji was also seen as a valuable adviser and team member, putting his Tata colleagues and employees before himself. Although he was comfortable working behind the scenes, offering guidance and leadership, Nowroji was not shy about speaking his mind. That combination of respect, leadership and flexibility brought him into Tata's inner circle, and he worked alongside Dorabji. Because of that close working relationship, no one was surprised when he was approached to succeed Dorabji as chairman upon his death in 1932.

A Leader for the People

Nowroji's leadership style was shaped by his experiences rising through the ranks of the mill workers at Tata. Always concerned for the well-being of his fellow employees, he pushed for benefits that were virtually unheard of during the early 1900s, including an innovative profit-sharing programme.

'For some time, we have been thinking about a method of associating the employees of the company more definitely with its prosperity in good times,'[1] Nowroji is recorded as saying to a Tata official at the time. 'You will be glad to hear that the board shares our views that we ought to show our employees our appreciation of their work when the company can afford to do so. Will you give full publicity to this [profit-sharing scheme] among all employees and let them know that it is the sincere wish of the company as a whole that its employees should share properly in its prosperity.'[2]

---

[1] 'The man who played from the heart'; available online at: http://www.tata.com/aboutus/articlesinside/CPKdkBZjW3c=/TLY-Vr3YPkMU=.
[2] Ibid.

Continuing on his reforming crusade, Nowroji instituted higher wages for Tata's lowest-paid workers in 1937 as well as improved conditions for temporary contractors at Tata Steel. Later, he introduced a club and recreation rooms for employees at Tata headquarters in Bombay House, so that workers would have a place to relax and enjoy some fitness activities.

Battling the Great Depression

Taking the helm during the worst global depression ever experienced, Nowroji saw cost-cutting and consolidation as his most urgent task. Doing more with less became the mantra across the board. He focused first on Tata's core businesses: iron and steel, mills, banking and power, and then turned to aid, through consolidation, several Indian cement businesses which were in turmoil. Although Tata was not in the cement business, it recognized that it was nevertheless a major player in Indian growth and construction.

Businessman F.E. Dinshaw had proposed a merger of the companies for the sake of their continued survival, but, unfortunately, he died in 1936, leaving the merger up in the air. Eager to be of assistance, Nowroji stepped in to try and broker the deal. He started by trying to identify the various companies' common interests and then worked through their differences, negotiating an agreement that was acceptable to all. Thanks to his diplomacy, the businesses merged to form Associated Cement Companies—one of Nowroji's proudest accomplishments.

Taking Care of Others

While Nowroji was mainly known as an advocate for Tata workers, his servant leadership extended far beyond Tata's reach. He was instrumental in proposing a cancer institute to serve all of India and directed funds from the Sir Dorabji Tata Trust—of which he was chairman—to that end.

He also devoted himself to turning around the poor financial condition of the Cricket Club of India. His success led to an improved reputation and the hope of longevity for the beleaguered club. Nowroji had actually been the first chairman of the club from its inception in

1933 until his death, and was heavily involved in the development and funding of Brabourne Stadium.

A number of honours came to him in recognition of his public service. He was made Justice of the Peace in 1917 and received the Order of the India Empire in 1923. He was knighted in 1933 and was made a Knight Commander of the Order of the British Empire in 1937.

Nowroji died suddenly of a heart attack in France in 1938, just six years after assuming the chairmanship. J.R.D. Tata, son of Ratanji Tata, Jamsetji's first cousin, was elected to succeed him. At thirty-four, he was the youngest chairman of the largest industrial group in India.

FOUR

J.R.D. TATA

J.R.D. Tata will forever be known for his obsession with aviation, but his early experiences growing up in Europe may have shaped his view of the Tata companies and of India, allowing him to ponder globalization long before chairmen of other corporations did so. Expansion was clearly the leading theme of JRD's tenure as chairman, and it greatly benefited the several Tata trusts that were established to more effectively distribute the wealth the company created.

Following the death of Tata chairman Nowroji Saklatwala in 1938, Jamsetji Tata's nephew, the leadership of the Tata Group passed to the next generation. Jamsetji

Tata's cousin's son Jehangir Ratanji Dadabhoy Tata—
JRD—took the helm. With the company having passed
through several years of financial struggle, JRD's mission
was expansion. And expand the company he did. Under
what would be a fifty-three-year chairmanship, the
business grew from fourteen companies to ninety-five,
and assets ballooned from $100 million to more than
$5 billion. If being named head of the largest industrial
group in India at such a tender age put pressure on JRD
to succeed, he responded spectacularly.

JRD and the French Connection

Born in Paris in 1904 to a French mother, Suzanne
'Sooni' Brière, and a Parsi father, Ratanji Dadabhoy
Tata, JRD spent much of his childhood in France.
French was his first language, and he subsequently
became fluent in English, but he never achieved native
fluency in any Indian language. If being raised far from
India impeded his command of his ancestral language,
it nevertheless broadened his global vision.

It also affected his personal appearance. Unlike
Jamsetji, who always wore the traditional white

robe, cap and flowing beard, JRD possessed a clean-shaven chin, a trim Western hairstyle, and felt most comfortable in European-style suits. These externals notwithstanding, he and Jamsetji were nearly identical in their values, but not in all their interests. One of JRD's most memorable traits was a love of flying, a consuming passion that contributed to his corporate legacy. After taking an aerial joyride at the age of fifteen, JRD was hooked for life. He avidly followed the career of his friend and neighbour Louis Blériot, the great French aviator who, in 1909, was the first to fly across the English Channel. As soon as he could, JRD began taking flying lessons and soloed after only three and a half hours in the air with an instructor.

JRD was educated in France as well as in Japan and England. As a French national, he was required to perform service in the French military and was drafted into the army for a mandatory year. He took to the experience and actually wanted to extend his service beyond the required year, so that he could attend the French cavalry's world-renowned equestrian school. His father forbade him. Although JRD was disappointed at the time, the paternal intervention saved his life. Soon after JRD left the army, his entire regiment was killed while on expeditionary service in Morocco.

JRD's goal after his military stint was to attend Cambridge University to study engineering. Again, however, his father stepped in, insisting that he instead come to India to work in the family business. JRD obeyed, but failing to earn the college degree he coveted was said to have haunted him for the rest of his life, despite his long success as the head of the Tata Group. He joined the company in 1925, as the age of twenty-one, and was assigned as an unpaid apprentice. The following year, soon after his father died, JRD was elevated to the board of Tata Sons. Whether motivated by his father's passing or his newly discovered love of India, JRD renounced his French citizenship in 1929 and gave his heart to the country his father had loved so much.

Piloting Planes and Companies

While learning everything there was to learn about his family's business was important to him, JRD continued to pursue his flying career. In 1929, he became India's very first recipient of a pilot's licence. Just three years later, in 1932, he founded the nation's first commercial airline, Tata Airlines, with an investment of 200,000 rupees (about $45,000 in today's times) from Tata Sons, which was sufficient to purchase two second-hand airplanes.

The pilot of the first commercial flight ever made in India was none other than JRD, who personally flew a cargo of mail from Karachi to Bombay. By the end of its first full year of operation, Tata Airlines' three pilots (JRD among them) transported 155 passengers and nearly 11 tons of mail a total of 160,000 miles. In 1946, Tata Airlines went public and was renamed Air-India Ltd. Two years later, in 1948, JRD founded Air-India International, the nation's first international airline. Five years after this, the Indian government nationalized Air-India—much to JRD's dismay. He was, however, appointed chairman of Air-India International and made a director of the board of Indian Airlines, the country's domestic carrier. Under his leadership, Air-India rose to global prominence.

Nationalized or not, Air-India was always his baby—his first love—and JRD remained on the board for twenty-five years. In recognition of his contributions to Indian aviation, JRD was given the title of Honorary Air Commodore of the Indian Air Force in 1966, and was promoted to Honorary Air Vice-Marshall in 1974. It was perhaps his proudest honour.

To be sure, JRD took over as Tata chairman with less experience than his predecessors, yet his moral compass was totally aligned with theirs. Like Jamsetji, Dorabji and Nowroji, he was committed to succeeding without stooping to the unethical behaviour all too common in the enterprises of developing countries—the use of bribery and the black market. Such practices, he made clear, would never be the Tata way. Fair and honest were his watchwords.

Success Breeds Success

Although JRD was a member of the Tata family, he recognized that Tata Sons could not realize its full potential for expansion and profit if it continued strictly as a family business. He therefore boldly broke with tradition and, instead of automatically putting family members in charge of the many Tata companies, he hired the best of the best. He wasn't afraid to pay for talent, either. He once joked that the Chinese chef he had hired to work at the Taj Mahal Hotel earned more than he did—and that, he believed, was precisely as it should be.

Of course, there was a downside to handing over authority to outsiders. Over time, disputes arose that threatened Tata's growth and ongoing success. Fortunately for the chairman and his firm, however, JRD knew when and where to take back control.

One company that grew notably under his leadership was Tata Chemicals. In 1939, JRD purchased an Indian chemical manufacturer that had been founded in the 1920s. Transforming it into a Tata company had its challenges, including the bombing of a cargo vessel transporting raw materials to its plant, but, as usual, JRD persevered. Still, it was 1944 before soda ash production began, with an initial capacity of 80 tons per day. Today, Tata Chemicals' soda ash plant produces 2500 tons per day, making it the second-largest producer in India.

In addition to Tata Chemicals, JRD initiated, expanded, purchased or led the way for such key Tata companies as Tata Electric, Tata Motors, Titan Industries, the cosmetics company Lakmé, Voltas (a major marketing, engineering and manufacturing firm), Tata Global Beverages, Tata Exports (today called Tata International), Tata Precision Industries and TCS—often described as the 'jewel in the crown' of the Tata companies.

Philanthropist-in-Training

Even before rising in the Tata Sons hierarchy, JRD was named trustee of the Sir Dorab Tata Trust in 1932. Coming so early in his career, his involvement in philanthropic work likely influenced his bold and energetic leadership style at the head of the firm. As key decision-maker for the trust, JRD was instrumental in establishing in 1941 the Tata Memorial Centre for Cancer Research and Treatment—the Bombay region's very first cancer hospital. Under his direction, the trust also funded the Tata Institute of Social Sciences in 1936, the Tata Institute of Fundamental Research in 1945, and the National Centre for the Performing Arts in 1966.

While JRD laboured to improve conditions for all Indians, he was especially concerned for the welfare of Tata employees. Through the years, he instituted internal policies to care of and protect the company's workers. He also created programmes to provide free medical care, retirement funding and workers' compensation. In 1979, Tata Steel took the radical step of legally stipulating that Tata workers were in the company's employ from the moment they left home for work until they returned home again. This extended worker liability insurance coverage was, in a manner, almost unthinkable even among the most enlightened employers of today.

Like his predecessors, JRD was passionate about improving the lives of the people who worked for the company. In a firm as large and complex as Tata, JRD could hardly establish a relationship with each and every employee, but he gave his full attention to whomever he spoke or interacted with. Such, certainly, was the case one afternoon when JRD, then in his late eighties, stopped to wish his younger sister Rodabeh Sawhney health, wealth and prosperity on the Parsi New Year. She was, at the time, widowed and living alone in the

Taj Mahal Hotel. While JRD was with her, the hotel housekeeper summoned the courage to suggest to him that perhaps his sister could be moved to a sea-facing room, which would give her the opportunity to watch the bustling activity on the water.

'I'm sure the hotel would not charge extra for it,' she assured JRD.

The remark rubbed him the wrong way. 'What do you mean the hotel would not charge extra for it?' he demanded. 'The Tatas do charity, they do not take charity!'

The housekeeper was mortified. But if she had the rest of her shift to ponder her gaffe, apparently so did the Tata chairman. When the housekeeper left work that evening, a car was waiting at the back gate. JRD was at the wheel.

'I wanted to apologize for my outburst,' he told her. 'May I drop you to your home this evening?' Pulling up to her house, he told her, 'I didn't want you to have a miserable evening thinking about the incident. Good night.'[1]

---

[1] Malavika Sangghvi, 'Saying sorry in style', Mid-day, 19 August

Most leaders would not have given the exchange that afternoon a second thought. The man's life story is filled with many similar anecdotes.

Parallel Goals

Like Jamsetji Tata, JRD viewed the future success of Tata Sons as inextricably linked with that of India. He was thoroughly committed to helping India achieve progress in education, in the eradication of poverty, in quality of life, and in health. He donated a sizeable portion of his personal wealth to establish some of the best research facilities and educational institutions in the nation. Among the organizations JRD endowed was the Tata Institute of Fundamental Research, which he helped establish in 1945. Its mission was to become a scientific institution to rival the best in the world, as well as to discover and share beneficial findings with India. It was not founded solely as a research institute, but as a means of actually delivering the benefits of scientific breakthroughs to a large population.

2013; available online at: http://www.mid-day.com/articles/saying-sorry-in-style/227569.

Curtailing Population Growth

One of JRD's biggest concerns for India was its out-of-control population growth. Whereas Prime Minister Nehru believed India's population was its greatest strength, JRD saw the connection between overpopulation and poverty, and he worked to reverse the trend. He donated generously to the study of population control, and founded what would later be named the International Institute of Population Studies. For this and all his years of work towards population control, JRD received the United Nations Population Award in 1992.

Like Jamsetji and Dorabji before him, JRD was an ardent supporter of women's rights long before it was a widely accepted cause in India, and he put his beliefs on the issue into direct action. In 1974, Sudha Murty was earning her master's degree in computer science at the Indian Institute of Science—the only woman in her postgraduate department and one of the top students in the programme. She was considering accepting an offer to earn her PhD in the US, when she happened to read an ad on a campus bulletin board for a job at Telco, today's Tata Motors. The notice infuriated her. Telco was looking to hire young, hardworking engineers with excellent grades—yet the last line of the ad specified: 'Lady candidates need not apply.'

Murty understood that as a female computer scientist, she was a rarity—and not just in India—at the time. But she had never faced so blatant an instance of gender discrimination. Livid, she fired off a letter to Telco to let them know what she thought of their anti-females policy. It was not that she actually wanted the job, but she was incensed that she was being excluded from consideration solely on account of her gender. She didn't know who was in charge, but she did know that J.R.D. Tata was the chairman of Tata Sons. And so she addressed a postcard to him, chastising him for allowing such discrimination to occur.

About a week after she posted her missive, Murty received a telegram inviting her to an all-expenses-paid interview at Telco's offices in Pune. Stunned, she gave in to the urging of her friends and accepted the offer.

As she seated herself before a committee of six, she overheard one of the members say, 'This is the girl who wrote to JRD.' Assuming this was a fatal mark against her, she decided she had nothing to lose and answered the committee's questions rather flippantly. To her amazement, at the end of the interview, she was told the job was hers if she wanted it.[2]

Sudha Murty had never met the man, but J.R.D. Tata had surely changed her life. His goal, however, was to change the lives of many. In pursuit of the same, he set up the J.R.D. Tata Trust in 1944. A few years later, he sold some of his shares in Tata as well as an apartment in Bombay, to fund the J.R.D. and Thelma Tata Trust, which is dedicated specifically to improving the lives of India's disadvantaged women. He and his wife, Thelma, never had children—though it is said that JRD seemed more comfortable around them than he appeared to be in the company of any adult.

Well-Deserved Recognition

For his efforts to improve the working and living conditions of Tata employees and customers as well

---

[2] 'Appro JRD', August 2004; available online at: http://www.tata.com/aboutus/articlesinside/UxG8Uwjyiks=/TLYVr3YPkMU=.

as all Indians, JRD earned a long list of honours. In 1955, he received the Padma Vibhushan, the second-highest civilian honour awarded by India. In 1988, it was a Guggenheim Medal for aviation and, in 1992, the Bharat Ratna, India's highest civilian honour, as well as the United Nations Population Award for his work initiating and furthering India's family planning movement.

JRD died at the age of eighty-nine in Geneva in 1993, and was interred at Père Lachaise Cemetery in his native Paris. In India, on the day of his passing, Parliament was adjourned—an honour typically reserved for former leaders of Parliament. Every member of that body knew, however, that JRD's influence had reached farther and had achieved more for India than most of India's politicians.

FIVE

RATAN TATA

Ratan Naval Tata assumed the top spot at Tata in 1991, following years of rapid expansion under JRD. Couple that growth with JRD's tendency to delegate, and you get a company with many, many little empires. In a climate of high autonomy and little coordination among the various Tata companies, Ratan introduced new controls to ensure that all the companies upheld the lofty standards of the group.

The year 1991 was a turning point for Tata Sons. Not only did J.R.D. Tata retire, turning over the reins to Ratan Tata, but Indian economic reforms were also enacted, opening many doors for the company outside of

India. It was Ratan's challenge to determine how best to take advantage of them. If the era of JRD's stewardship was known mainly for vigorous but conservative growth in India, Ratan's reign was all about global expansion, often through acquisition. When he took over in 1991, Tata Sons was a $5 billion business. At his retirement, twenty-one years later, the conglomerate's revenues had climbed to almost $100 billion. The growth strategy was a combination of entering new industry sectors, buying companies and acquiring controlling stakes in yet others.

Ratan's father, Naval Tata, was Jamsetji's distant relative and had been adopted by Jamsetji's youngest son—also named Ratan—and his wife, Navajbai. Naval had three sons, of whom Ratan was the eldest. Educated in India through secondary school, he attended college and graduate school in the United States, earning a BS in architecture from Cornell University in 1962, and completing the Advanced Management Programme at Harvard in 1975. After graduating from Cornell, Ratan returned to India to begin work at Tata on the shop floor—literally—of Tata Steel. He shovelled limestone and tended the blast furnace. Ratan rose through the ranks and, in 1991, when JRD announced that he was stepping down as chairman, he personally designated Ratan as his successor. Ratan had worked closely with JRD for many years, and was the chairman of Tata Industries and on the board of Tata Motors, so JRD knew he was leaving Tata in the safe hands of someone who had spent some thirty years in the company.

Retaking Control

Ratan took the helm of what had become a collection of highly autonomous companies, thanks to the tendency of the ageing JRD to spend less time on day-to-day business matters and to allow business unit managers more and more decision-making responsibility. Independence became—and still is—a hallmark of the Tata companies. While that can be a very good thing, too much independence can also be dangerous and difficult, especially when a new chairman endeavours to introduce new policies and procedures. Not surprisingly, Ratan faced resistance from company heads when he tried to institute some major changes aimed at centralizing certain aspects of management and policy.

Ratan understood that, given the culture JRD had created, he could not simply rule by fiat. To re-establish productive ties with the various companies and impress upon them the need for pulling together in productive cooperation, Ratan decided to invest financially in each company, thereby increasing Tata Sons' direct control.

Ratan also had his hands on another lever of control. By the time he became chairman, the Tata family's direct ownership stake in Tata Sons had fallen to just 1.5 per cent. Ratan was, however, chairman of the philanthropic trusts that held majority stakes in the Tata companies. This gave Ratan significant, albeit indirect, control of the firm's destiny.

Unifying the Brand

Nothing in the Tata playbook ever came down to pure finance. For Tata, money was important, but far from all-important. In addition to acquiring a strategic financial stake in key companies, Ratan Tata promulgated, in 1998, a Code of Conduct that served to unite the sometimes contentious Tata business units in adherence to a common set of ethical values. Indeed, nothing more powerfully exemplifies what differentiates Tata from its peers and competitors than the Tata Code of Conduct (TCoC). Every employee of every company in the group that shares the Tata name must sign the TCoC. (You can read this remarkably thoughtful and insightful document in its entirety in Appendix B of this book.) Had investment bankers, insurance executives, mortgage lenders, and members of the US Congress signed on to such a document, one wonders if the global financial crisis that took hold in 2008 would even have been possible.

While the TCoC did much to make everyone in the far-flung Tata empire conscious of their common ethical identity and purpose, Ratan also instituted a corporate branding initiative designed to reposition Tata Sons as innovative and forward-thinking, and to make it clearer which companies constituted the Tata core. Essentially, Ratan set out to use the highly valued Tata brand to bring divergent companies back into the corporate fold. Instead of imposing the Tata name on affiliated businesses, each business had to earn the right to use it.

The first and most important step towards earning that right was signing on to the Brand Equity and

Business Promotion Agreement (BEBPA). This was a detailed agreement outlining the business principles that all Tata companies wanting to use the Tata brand had to sign up for. Included in the BEBPA was a requirement that employees of the Tata companies sign the TCoC. Every year, the CEO of every Tata company has to sign a compliance report confirming adherence to the BEBPA.

Beginning in 1998, each and every company in the group had to embrace the code fully. If a company chose not to sign and agree to the terms of the code, Tata Sons could divest itself of any ownership stake in that company. Whatever a company leader's desire for autonomy, it did not trump respect for the long-established value of the Tata name. To sever ties with such a brand could mean financial disaster.

Those companies that signed the TCoC and reaffirmed their Tata identity displayed a newly developed Tata logo, which marked the firm as part of the Tata conglomerate. The Tata name was also brought out from behind a welter of acronyms that had proliferated among some companies in the group, but that did not effectively leverage the Tata reputation. Companies like the Tata Iron and Steel Company and Telco (Tata

Engineering and Locomotive Company) were renamed Tata Steel and Tata Motors, respectively. In a few cases, it was decided that the brand of a particular business could beneficially stand alone. The most notable instance was the Taj Hotels chain, into which the Tata name was never inserted. A few newer and potentially riskier ventures were also strategically kept at arm's length by withholding from them the Tata name.

Signing the BEBPA obligated the companies to pay to the Tata Group 0.15–0.25 per cent of the annual revenues, subject to a cap of 5 per cent of profits, a sum that was reinvested in marketing and promoting the Tata parent brand. Overall, however, Ratan's efforts to create a common set of expectations and practices and to collect promotional funds has served to keep the Tata brand strong in the eyes of consumers and business-to-business partners, and has been very helpful in persuading the companies to pull together.

Expanding the Tata Footprint

During his tenure, Ratan employed a variety of methods to add a wide range of companies and products to the

Tata Group. Among these were the establishment of Tata Teleservices; the acquisition of Tetley Tea; the debut of the Indica, India's first domestically designed and manufactured car; the formation of a joint venture with the American International Group (AIG) to allow Tata's re-entry into the insurance industry; obtaining a controlling stake in Videsh Sanchar Nigam Ltd (now called Tata Communications); forming Tata Indicom mobile service and launching Tata Sky satellite television service; unveiling the Ginger hotel chain; nurturing TCS to more than $10 billion in revenue; building Tata Housing, a pioneer in low-cost housing; acquiring part of Daewoo Motors and steel-maker Corus; acquiring Jaguar and Land Rover; and partnering with Starbucks in India. These are just some of many other acquisitions, joint ventures and new product launches.

Even before he was named chairman, Ratan pushed for investment in global entrepreneurial ventures, with the goal of ultimately bringing the resulting technology to India. In the early 1980s, he advocated for an investment in start-up technologies in parallel computing. In such initiatives, Ratan usually received the enthusiastic support of JRD, the chairman at the time.

Once Ratan became chairman himself, the Internet was beginning to come into its own. The new Tata leader was quick to grasp the potential of the new online technology, and he embraced it enthusiastically and creatively.

Making Good on Promises

The Tata reputation for honesty and trustworthiness has stood the test of time. Its name and brand are virtually synonymous with trust. So, in 2002, when, in the wake of a major loss, certain irregularities came to light in financial paperwork filed by Tata Finance, Ratan had two options. He could take care of things internally, cover the losses and deal very quietly with those involved. Or, he could opt for transparency and full disclosure, letting the public know that Tata would not tolerate anything unethical or illegal.

He chose the latter, publicly disclosing the situation and announcing that he was commissioning an independent audit of Tata Finance. The result was the discovery of a range of inappropriate, even criminal, activities, from insider trading to filing false paperwork.

Ratan hid none of it, and the press, predictably, had a field day. Ratan could only watch as the Tata name was dragged through the mud for several weeks. Yet, he felt strongly that the guilty had to be punished, and Tata Sons had to be absolutely honest with the public about what had happened.

Indeed, Ratan went far beyond disclosure. He met with investors specifically to address the situation at Tata Finance. He met with the various banks, including the Reserve Bank of India.[1] He revealed to the stakeholders that problems with accounting had been discovered and that, instead of the huge profits that had been reported for years, Tata Finance was actually operating at a loss. He confessed that, at this point, he did not know the extent of the losses. As that sunk in, he made a pledge. Whatever their magnitude, the losses would be covered 100 per cent. No investor would lose any money.

Ratan could easily—and legally—have disclaimed responsibility. Tata Finance was, after all, a limited

---

[1] Michael C. Knap, *Contemporary Auditing: Real Issues & Cases* (Mason: South-Western Cengage Learning, 2009).

liability corporation, and plenty of other corporate leaders have wrapped themselves in the corporate veil.

But Ratan believed the company had a 'moral responsibility' to correct the problem, and he promised it would. Besides, he also believed that the Tata name was of almost incalculable value. Whatever the financial loss, the loss of the reputation behind this name would be totally unacceptable. Only a full financial guarantee would restore public faith in Tata.

At that, the cost was high—between Rs 5000–7000 million ($81–114 million) to cover Tata Finance's losses. Yet, the honesty and responsibility this payout demonstrated was an investment worth many times that amount. Instead of having to patch up a battered reputation, Tata emerged from the crisis looking better than before.

Protecting the People

Although Tata Sons is a profitable enterprise, it does not —and never did—exist primarily for profit. It exists— first and foremost—to improve the lives of the people of

India and, now that remit has been expanded globally, especially those who work for its companies, live in the shadow of its factories and buy its products. The Tata Nano, one of the least expensive cars in the world, came into being because Ratan feared for the women and children, who were riding through Mumbai's streets, piled high on ubiquitous and unprotected two-wheeled motor scooters. He saw the need for an enclosed car that would allow families to travel together through the streets safely—and without requiring a mortgage to purchase. Rather than see families risk their lives, Ratan challenged Tata Motors to develop a car that would be compact, safe and affordable for the typical Indian family.

The challenge was accepted and, in 2009, Tata Motors debuted the Nano, one of the smallest cars ever manufactured, with a sticker price equivalent to about $1500. At the time of its launch, it was India's most affordable and lowest-cost passenger car. The price has inched up since 2009, but the project has been a success because it meets a critical need.

The imperative to protect the people is active and heroic throughout Tata, at every level and to a remarkable degree. On 26 November 2008, a series of terrorist attacks rocked Mumbai. Among the targets was the Taj Mahal Hotel, Jamsetji Tata's iconic gift to the people and spirit of India. For three days and two nights, the Taj was under siege as terrorists stalked the halls of the grand old hotel, shooting people, starting fires, detonating plastic explosive charges, tossing grenades, and relentlessly creating horror and chaos.

There were approximately 500 registered guests and about 600 others dining in the hotel or attending various banquets and functions. Serving the guests were some 600 staff members, many very young, many the sole breadwinners of their families. As employees, all of them knew the back doorways, the hidden passages and the escape routes in the hotel. The expected action, the natural impulse, would be flight. But not one of the staff members fled. Not one. Some helped guests to escape and then re-entered the hotel to help others. Hotel telephone operators, evacuated early in the attack, all volunteered to return, and they stayed on duty all night, serving as the hub of communication, calling each room to warn guests and give them vital survival instructions. Other staff members did all they could to keep guests both calm and safe. They protected their guests throughout the long attack and were instrumental in saving people from the fires that engulfed parts of the Taj. As one twenty-four-year-old woman, a hotel banquet manager, explained, 'Well, I was scared, but there was something more important that needed to be done. Because I was there, because I was looking after the function, I was responsible. I could have been the youngest in the room, but I was still doing my job.'

'The easiest thing for a staff member to do at that point in time was to drop whatever they were doing and run out of the hotel. Not one did that,' Abhijit Mukherji, executive director of hotel operations, observed. In fact, many did much more. Kitchen employees, including senior chefs, formed a human chain to usher guests to safety. The terrorists came upon this evacuation in progress and attacked, gunning down six of the chefs, who took bullets intended for their guests.

When I met with Mr Tata to discuss the book, he said, 'Peter, I can't explain it. There were no manuals, no instructions for what should be done in these circumstances. So what seems to have happened is that individuals, from the waiters to the managers of the restaurants, all had this goal of "Let's get the guests to safety."' Of about 1700 people in the hotel, more than 1600 escaped safely. Of the thirty-four people killed, twelve were staff members, another seven of whom were injured.

Harvard Business School professor Rohit Deshpande found three lessons in the response of the Taj employees to the attack on their hotel. He learned that Tata recruited hotel employees from high schools in small towns rather than big cities. They were recruited less for their academic grades than for their demonstrated attitude of respect. The company then trained front-line staff, not to be ambassadors for the Tata brand, but to be ambassadors for the guest. Each staff member is actually called a 'guest ambassador', whose principal job it is to be the voice of the guest to the company. Most importantly, incentives are not just based on salary, but on recognition for service and excellence. And so the performance of Taj staff during the hotel's darkest hours stands today as a beacon of hope, and the product of a unique and uniquely motivated way of doing business in the world.

Passing the Torch

I remember the first time I heard Ratan Tata speak. It was at the launch of the Small Business Unit of TCS in 2011, which was headed up by a friend of mine named Swamy, who introduced Ratan to an audience of 500 VIPs. I expected the chairman would deliver the 'thank you all for coming' address that is customary on such occasions. After all, he was chairman of many of the Tata companies and was a phenomenally busy person. I hardly expected a detailed technical analysis of where the industry was, where it was going, and how TCS would be the leader. But that is exactly what Ratan delivered.

He spoke for twenty-five minutes without notes and in great detail. When he was finished, he answered questions. His command of specifics and particulars was amazing. The gentleman sitting next to me said quietly, 'He can speak with equal authority on every company on which he sits on the board!'

Ratan was the chairman of the Tata Group from 1991 until he retired in December 2012. He now holds the title of Chairman Emeritus and continues to be active in the company as an adviser. He has also remained in charge of the trusts. The new Tata Group chairman, Cyrus Mistry, worked with Ratan for a year as deputy chairman, watching and learning how Tata does business. Cyrus had also been on the board of Tata since 2006 and had been on the boards of other Tata companies, so he was exceptionally qualified to take over the reins from Ratan.

SIX

TATA CONSULTANCY SERVICES

TCS is a case study in how Tata builds successful companies. Tata typically starts in market niches where there is less completion or a lower barrier to entry. Next, the company invests in capabilities, people and relationships. It works to move into more profitable lines of businesses, either through expansion, acquisition, or by creating entirely new lines of business. TCS is now among the highest valued companies in its industry globally, and is deemed the jewel in the Tata crown.

Of the Tata Group's 130-plus businesses, TCS is today the most prominent and most valuable. Providing

IT services, consulting and business solutions, TCS is also currently the most profitable of all the Tata companies. Its success has helped to shore up or fund growth in other Tata ventures, all the while moving quickly upmarket in an extremely competitive consulting environment and operating as one of the fastest-growing IT services companies in the world.

That hasn't always been the case. A few years ago, TCS was stuck at the bottom of the IT consulting pyramid. Having started at ground level as an operations consulting firm specializing in day-to-day IT management, TCS quickly became a major player in that space. Operations consulting is, however, a low-margin, low-prestige business, and TCS had visions of providing far more than this limited level of consulting offerings. Like its Tata brethren, it aspired to greatness.

Thus driven, within a few short years, TCS moved into managing IT infrastructure, transaction processing and offering its global clients consulting-led solutions that it would implement, operate and support successfully. Now highly competitive with these and other consultancies, TCS rose by building expertise in a number of core competencies and then skilfully marketing that knowledge to other companies. It currently employs over 300,000 workers in forty-six countries and expects to hire 55,000 more during the financial year 2014. That is rapid growth.

Today, TCS is the largest Indian company based on market capitalization. It is also the largest India-based IT services company, and was named in the *Forbes* list of the world's most innovative companies. It recently passed the $60 billion market-capitalization mark, surpassing major rival Accenture.

A Backward Glance

TCS is rooted in the internal IT resource J.R.D. Tata created in 1968. Quite quickly, the unit transitioned to providing services to external as well as internal clients. Early contracts involved creating an inter-branch reconciliation system for the Central Bank of India. The breadth and depth of services grew from there, and under the leadership of Fakir Chand Kohli, an electrical engineer seconded from Tata Electric Companies, TCS launched, by 1975, a formal training programme for a dozen or so first-year recruits from the Indian Institute of Technology and the Indian Institute of Science, as a way to create a steady stream of talented and qualified IT candidates. The training programme remains a feeder of strong technical talent to this day; only the scale has increased, with TCS now spending over 15 million hours every year training its people.

Hiring the best and the brightest is a hallmark of Tata Sons, and TCS typifies the group-wide insistence on excellence. As former TCS CEO and current vice chairman Subramanian Ramadorai explained, in addition to finding pros with in-depth technical skills, 'We've always had passionate people, people who are all willing to roll up their sleeves and get down to brass tacks. They've performed relentlessly to help TCS reach milestone after milestone.' That willingness to assume responsibility and take action is quintessential Tata—and it is a rare commodity in today's large and complex corporations.

In 2004, three decades after Kohli—often dubbed the 'Father of Indian IT'—started building the academia–ecosystem for Indian IT to thrive, TCS was incorporated as a separate entity under the Tata Sons umbrella. As Tata recognized the coming opportunities in the software industry, it began positioning TCS for greater success. As is typical in the Tata corporate hierarchy, once divisions demonstrate productive self-sufficiency, they are pushed out of the nest to take wing as independent businesses. It is important to note that TCS was, at this time, a true entrepreneurial venture—small, but clever. Leveraging its independence fuelled its growth and ambition.

Attracting Top Talent

The key to the TCS strategy for success has always been an intensive, wide-ranging search for talent. TCS goes more than the proverbial extra mile to identify, attract and retain top consultants and analysts. Fortunately for the enterprise, once they join the Tata family, few employees ever want to leave. Pervading each company and the Tata Group as a whole is a sense and spirit of community—which brings employees together for activities inside and outside of work.

Feeling a part of the global community is even more important, however. The company's larger mission of helping others is a major draw for employees. They know—or quickly learn—that the Tatas have never been in the business just for the money. Because they are not evaluated solely by financial metrics, TCS employees are free and motivated to invest their time and energy in work they know will benefit others. It's an addictive way of life.

Beyond feeling the conviction that they play an important role in social change, TCS employees—like employees throughout the Tata Group—are well cared for. They are encouraged to participate in fitness and wellness activities on TCS campuses. The company enthusiastically supports employee sports at the local as well as national level.

TCS-Maitree was organized specifically to foster a spirit of camaraderie among TCS employees and their families through activities designed to encourage their hidden aspirations and talents, and to extend the TCS community into the larger community beyond the company. It is a platform for employee-initiated programmes—all in the Tata spirit of making life better for others. These programmes demonstrate that while salaries are highly competitive and the TCS employee health-care programme superb, financial incentives and other perks are perhaps not the only important reasons that associates join the TCS team.

Audaciously Big Goals

'Audaciously big' goals—that is how S. Ramadorai described the strategic targets the company aims for. Back in the late 1990s, the TCS team began meeting weekly at Ramadorai's house in Mumbai to create a vision for what TCS could be. Ramadorai was the visionary who sold Ratan Tata on what TCS could achieve. That vision included ambitious—audacious—financial goals.

'One of our first ideas was to get to Rs 2000 crore in revenues [approximately $320 million] by 2000,' says Ramadorai, 'simply because it looked achievable and had a nice ring to it. Soon, we realized it was too short a target.'

From that achievement came a new goal: 'Top 10 by 2010'. TCS challenged itself to become a top 10 IT software and services company by the end of the first decade of the new century. It was audacious, but also specific and doable. The goal quickly became the company's rallying cry.

But TCS didn't stop there. Management followed through on execution by taking steps to ensure the goal would be met. Top managers met regularly with employees during special open houses at which they would break down what each individual could do— and what teams needed to do together—to transform vision into accomplished fact. These conversations helped hone the critical activities that would have the greatest impact. They were the 'Top 10 by 2010' success parameters—revenue, profitability, number of employees and market capitalization. By 2003, TCS was a $1 billion IT services company. By 2009, it was at $6 billion, having cracked the top 10 list a year early. In 2013, it topped $11 billion, and still shows no sign of slowing down.

Clients and Prospects

While TCS always provided top-notch services, the company's sales and marketing capabilities were once perceived as weak—and quite rightly so. Accordingly, in early 2009, Natarajan Chandrasekaran (Chandra), at the time the designated CEO, decided to divide the company based on customer relationships. He split personnel into two groups—one he designated 'Sales', the other 'Client Partners'. Sales were the sales and business development professionals charged with finding or rebuilding customer relationships—and this group was further broken out by industry.

Chandra supported both groups by setting up global centres of excellence, which developed world-class solutions that the Sales could sell to new clients and the Client Partners could sell to the existing ones.

The new approach worked wonders. In just four years, TCS vaulted from a purveyor of operational IT services to a full-services firm with a portfolio of businesses spanning IT, IT infrastructure, Business Process Services—embedded with high-quality domain, technology and consulting talent. The company rose to the high end of the global consulting scale in a few short years, while still retaining its bread-and-butter business in IT services. Today, TCS competes at every level of the consulting value chain and is regarded as a full-service firm on par with IBM and Accenture.

Head-to-Head with the Biggest and the Best

By creating customer- and industry-focused units backed by focused centres of excellence and innovation across its key markets, Chandra built a new type of organization that was small enough to remain agile and relevant to customers in each market by being close to them, but also allowed these nimble units to leverage the powerhouse of technology and industry expertise that TCS had built.

The first centre, established in 2007, was the global consulting practice, the GCP. Subsequently, in Peterborough, England, TCS set up the first insurance solution centre of excellence. Today, there are sixteen centres of excellence, operating out of the United States, Australia, Argentina, Columbia, Spain, the Netherlands, Hungary, South Africa, Singapore, China and South Korea. Allowed to focus exclusively on their specialty, each centre of excellence has developed deep expertise along with a reputation for producing results. This approach has helped TCS develop a breadth and depth of subject-area expertise that has allowed the company to go head-to-head against the older, most established consulting firms.

An Obsession with Doing Things Right

With its climbing market capitalization, TCS has drawn applause from analysts and clients alike. 'TCS has long been the 800-pound gorilla in the Indian offshore space, but until recently has never really been able to take its rightful spot in the market, always overshadowed by the likes of Infosys and Wipro,' says Partha Iyengar, Gartner Research Head in India. 'Today, they have very clearly separated themselves from the rest of the Indian pack.'

While Iyengar was speaking about TCS, the assessment holds true for nearly all of the Tata companies. Tata Sons is run like no other enterprise on earth. And that is a good thing—for all of us. An obsession with doing things the right way, coupled with a passion for charitable work, has been passed down through the decades from Jamsetji at the very inception of the firm. This ethos continues to energize and challenge company employees to do the very best work they can—not for themselves and for the prospect of a raise or promotion, but because it will generate more profits to be invested in doing good by improving many lives. How many other for-profit companies are dedicated essentially to making more and more money, so that they have more to give away?

None. Tata Sons stands alone in its mission and its operating principles. It stands alone, but it could well serve as a role model for the most deeply ambitious among us.

The first Chairman, Jamsetji Tata (1839–1904)

The second Chairman, Sir Dorabji Tata (1859–1932)

Sir Ratan Tata (1871–1918)

The third Chairman, Sir Nowroji Saklatwala (1875–1938)

The fourth Chairman, J.R.D. Tata (1904–93)

The fifth Chairman, Ratan Tata (1937–)

The sixth and current chairman of the Tata Group,
Cyrus Pallonji Mistry (1968–)

PART II

THE TATA DNA

SEVEN

THE ORIGINS OF TATA PHILANTHROPHY

The Parsi faith has profoundly influenced the Tata family, bringing concern for the needs of others to the fore.

Legend has it that around the eighth–tenth century, a small group of persecuted Persians migrated to a city, north of where Mumbai now is, to practise their religion in peace. The land was ruled by the king Jadi Rana, who was reluctant to allow a group of foreigners to settle in his kingdom for fear they would overburden the area's resources. He sent the leader of the refugees a full bowl of milk to signify that the land they were on was already full and could support no more.

Understanding the message, the refugee leader added some sugar to the bowl and sent it back to the king. The brilliant metaphor instantly won over Jadi Rana. He allowed the Parsis to stay—and, true to the promise of the metaphor, they worked hard, never to burden the community, but only to sweeten or enrich it.

This section of the book investigates the ethical drivers of this unique enterprise—call it the Tata DNA. It includes a commitment to philanthropy—not as an adjunct to business, but as the *reason* for business.

To understand the Tata family's deep commitment to philanthropy—and, in particular, its application in India—we have to understand something of the religion from which the family sprang. India's Parsi community, though small, lives by a clear edict: improve society. The Tatas have made this their life's work.

The Parsi Religion

While the modern-day Parsi community originated in Persia (today's Iran) and immigrated to India generations ago, the Zoroastrian religion on which the community's faith was founded predates Christianity, Judaism and Islam. In fact, dating at least to the second millennium BCE, it is the earliest monotheistic religion of which we have any knowledge.

Zarathustra—also known as Zoroaster—may have lived anytime between the eighteenth and sixth centuries BCE. At fifteen, he decided to devote his life to the worship of God. Five years later, he left the pleasures of society to meditate alone in a cave, pondering the big questions of life, such as the origin of evil, why we are here, and how the universe came to exist. In his solitude, his God, Ahura Mazda, appeared to him. The two conducted a dialogue, which led Zarathustra to write the Gathas, the sacred verses of Zoroastrianism.

Zoroastrianism is an activist faith, its adherents accepting a commitment to fight evil, which reveals itself in such physical forms as poverty, hunger, disease, suffering, crime, greed and prejudice—in short, virtually all the ills of human society. The religious duty of each man and woman is to work towards the eradication of evil in all its varieties. As Noshir Dadrawala of the Centre for Advancement of Philanthropy says, 'Parsi

Thy Name is Charity. If Christ asked his followers to love their neighbours, Zarathustra asked his followers to attain happiness by making others happy.'

People of Commerce

A poor people when they settled in India, the Parsis rose in prominence during the seventeenth century, when they opened trading posts that did a great deal of business with Europeans. The Parsis not only welcomed the trade, they were eager to learn from their European partners, and they very quickly developed both a passion and skill for commerce. This motivated the community to move closer to the commercial action, which, as the seventeenth century gave way to the eighteenth, was Bombay—modern Mumbai. Indeed, the activity of Parsi merchants did much to accelerate the growth and affluence of Bombay through the eighteenth and nineteenth centuries. By the 1800s, thanks in no small measure to the Parsi community, parts of the city grew wealthy—as did the Parsi people of business. They, in turn, invested much of their wealth in major modes of transportation, especially railways and shipbuilding, which helped fuel India's entry into global commerce, while further enriching the Parsi community. The Parsi people did well by doing good, and everyone benefited.

Where some individuals work hard to build strictly personal wealth, Parsis work hard to make a greater contribution to the community at large. They earn and build in order to effect large-scale change rather than create lavish individual lifestyles. They are doers who feel a personal responsibility to leave the world a better place than it was when they came into it. To make a positive change in even one single life, they believe, is to have lived a successful life oneself.

Today, there are approximately 70,000 Parsis in India. Modest as these numbers are, they are also dwindling. The Western trend of marrying later in life and having fewer children may well bring the Parsis to the brink of extinction as a group.

Parsi Culture

In addition to their religious beliefs, members of the Parsi community share certain interests and hobbies, among which are health and fitness. Often compared to Californians in their interest in (some would say obsession with) alternative medicine, Parsis work hard at keeping themselves in optimal shape. Being health-conscious does not mean that they deprive themselves of the finer things in life, however. Parsis are considered foodies, with an avid preference for dining at the best restaurants and using the freshest ingredients in preparing meals at home. They love life and live it to the fullest—without being ostentatious about it. This extends to their appreciation and support for the fine arts and the performing arts—and a passion for horse racing. The track in Mumbai is a Parsi gathering place.

Parsis are often enthusiastic fashionistas, with a taste for stylish clothing and chic home decor. They are not, however, narcissists. Their appreciation for what life has to offer is not to be confused with a worship of selfish pursuits. That is not what Parsi life is about. They are social activists who are committed to enjoying life while serving others.

The Parsi Influence on Jamsetji Tata

In the context of Mumbai's Parsi community, we return to Jamsetji Tata, one of the most famous and most highly respected latter-day Parsis. While the Parsi religion, culture and values have existed for centuries, never before had an entrepreneur taken Parsi tenets and applied them, as Jamsetji did, so intimately and specifically to business. As Jamsetji saw it, creating business organizations whose ultimate purpose was to fund ever-greater battles against sickness and poverty and hunger was God's work. He set out to start and then to grow profitable enterprises capable of generating revenues that could be invested in helping those less fortunate. Not only did Jamsetji reinvest in his businesses and his employees, but he also invested in their neighbourhoods and their environment. He worked to supply India with the power to fight evil by investing in education and health care and technology.

Jamsetji succeeded in business partly because of his relentless insistence on personal excellence—another Parsi value. Doing your best work and asking the same of others yields superior results. This was Jamsetji's mindset as he worked to build his companies and his country. When hiring managers or other key workers, he invariably searched out the best, most talented people he could find. He often travelled overseas in search of the right candidate for the job, and he did not hesitate to pay well for the expertise he needed. While he leveraged the talents of other nations, he also invested in the education and training of the best and brightest in India. His goal was a future in which he would not have to look beyond Mumbai for the talent his companies needed.

'There is one kind of charity common enough among us,' he said. 'It is that patchwork philanthropy which clothes the ragged, feeds the poor and heals the sick. I am far from decrying the noble spirit which seeks to help a poor or suffering fellow being. However, what advances a nation or a community is not so much to prop up its weakest and most helpless members, but to lift up the best and the most gifted, so as to make them of the greatest service to the country.'[1] This Jamsetji did by

---

[1] 'The quotable Jamsetji Tata', March 2008; available online at: http://www.tata.com/aboutus/articlesinside/1U2QamAhqtA=/ TLYVr3YPkMU=.

establishing scholarships, creating training programmes, and generally investing in the local workforce.

Looking After Others

When Jamsetji Tata founded his first company, his goal was not personal wealth and fortune. It was success for the benefit of India. Following his religion, he was moved to create a vehicle to serve the needy, who were—and still are—so abundant in India. He envisioned a social system in which the hiring of local workers would create jobs and income to enrich the local community, while the workers' contributions to the company would create revenue that would further enrich both the community and the country. His vision was simultaneously capitalist and socialist. And this hybrid was unique.

Whatever their religious origin, Jamsetji's philanthropic goals were driven and enabled by business. Thanks to mentoring by his father, Jamsetji was quickly able to start his own cotton mill, followed by other mills and textile businesses, energy companies, iron and steel mills, and so on. As he recognized a need or a business opportunity, Jamsetji planned a way to meet the need or realize the opportunity. In this, he was the quintessential entrepreneur. It was the way he applied his entrepreneurial skills to community development and philanthropy that set him apart.

Once his companies began generating a profit, Jamsetji created the groundwork for the establishment of philanthropic trusts. (Today, these trusts hold a 66 per cent ownership stake in Tata Sons.) In turn, the trusts have been responsible for creating national institutions to enrich Indian citizens. The Tata trusts have helped to fund numerous educational and social organizations, including those devoted to medical research, science and technology, social studies and performing arts.

While Jamsetji Tata's goal was always to improve the lives of all of the people of India, the approach was often immediate and local. Rather than import professional help, the Tatas typically chose to train and educate people in communities around new plants and facilities. Generous in their support of causes to help the needy, the Tata culture has always demanded the personal responsibility, accountability and wholehearted involvement of the recipients of their aid.

Unparalleled Patriotism

From the start of his entrepreneurial career, Jamsetji Tata aimed to build a successful business empire to enrich his country and his countrymen rather than himself. Having travelled internationally, Jamsetji—more than most Indians—saw and recognized the many opportunities his country had for improving the condition of its people. Seeing the ugly and unhealthy industrial towns that had sprung up around factories in England, Jamsetji conceived a vision of an improved industrial town design. Seeing the power of an American waterfall, he was inspired to bring hydroelectric power to Bombay. Staying in Europe's luxury hotels, he began thinking about the dearth of first-class, world-class hospitality establishments in Bombay and how their absence discouraged tourism as well as foreign business in India. He endeavoured to use each new experience and insight to inspire and create beneficial change in India.

Step one in actually executing the necessary transformation was an investment in the basics: heavy manufacturing, education, medicine and improved living conditions. Jamsetji saw that great strides in all of these areas were possible as long as adequate funding was available. So he made it his life's mission to ensure a steady flow of the capital necessary to pull India out of poverty.

The Role of Philanthropy

Although Tata frequently collaborates with and works through government agencies, public agencies often have to contend with constraints that do not bind private organizations. Think of it as the difference between a department of education deciding to issue laptops to all high school students—a programme that might take years to be approved and funded—and the Bill & Melinda Gates Foundation deciding to fund such an effort within a week.

Which organization will create results sooner? Money—and direct control over it—buys speed. Philanthropic trusts such as those of the Tatas are subject to fewer regulations, laws and constituencies. They have the natural licence to take more risks and try untested approaches to situations, whereas more conservative government agencies lack the will and the authority to do so. It is the freedom to act directly on the urgings of conscience and the immediate perception of values that makes large-scale change possible. In short, philanthropy makes the 'impossible' possible, very quickly.

EIGHT

THE TATA TRUSTS

The Tata trusts are a set of philanthropic trusts established by members of the Tata family, to which the majority of the family's personal wealth has been dedicated and bequeathed. The trusts now control 66 per cent of Tata, but have no direct involvement in the oversight or management of the company. They are unique in being owned by an organization dedicated to social service. There is a commission in India that oversees the management and governance of all charitable trusts.

Tata Sons has long been regarded as one of the most successful companies in history, and part of the reason for its success may well be its ownership structure. The Tata trusts—philanthropic trusts established by members of the Tata family, not mutual funds or pensions or even individual investors—ultimately control the global conglomerate. The Tata trusts were established for the express purpose of funnelling the personal wealth of the Tata family into social programmes to benefit the people.

Shernaz Vasunia, programme officer of the Sir Dorabji Tata Trust, explains: 'Over 75 per cent of our trust's funds come from dividends on the shares it owns in Tata Sons, the group's holding company. The remainder comes from their own statutory investments.'

Supporting Education

Philanthropy for education was a new concept when Jamsetji Tata created the first Tata trust, the J.N. Tata Endowment, in 1892. His goal was to help promising Indian students attend college, those who could not otherwise afford to do so. Six years later, Jamsetji set aside half his personal fortune for a research institute, the Indian Institute of Science, which opened its doors in

1911. Incidentally, two years after Jamsetji's pioneering gift, in 1900, Andrew Carnegie donated $1 million to found a 'technical school' in Pittsburgh, Pennsylvania, which would later become Carnegie Mellon University.

To date, the J.N. Tata Endowment has supported more than 3500 scholars. Many of the recipients have gone on to become scientists, doctors, writers, performing artists, and even an Indian president, K.R. Narayanan.

Jamsetji's first concept of philanthropy consisted of a 'patchwork' of giving, referring to a pattern of donating money here and there to causes that had immediate needs. That is how his life's work began, but he quickly realized that a patchwork approach would not achieve the large-scale results he desired, and so he developed what he called the constructive philanthropy approach, using his trusts to leverage, in service to the needy, the talents and skills of the best and most gifted. The Jamsetji Tata Trust was set up in 1974, long after the founder's death, to celebrate the centenary of his first company. It provides grants for innovation.

In the Founder's Footsteps

Like their father, Sir Dorabji and Sir Ratan Tata also donated the majority of their personal wealth to trusts they established. Since neither had children, their wealth could be dealt with in whole rather than divided among a progeny. Had they bequeathed shares in the business to children and grandchildren, the ownership of the company might have been fractured, with a detrimental effect on Tata Sons. By establishing trusts and placing their fortunes into these unifying financial structures, however, they helped to keep the company intact.

Sir Ratan funded a number of initiatives to benefit India in one way or another, from financing the first archaeological excavation at Pataliputra, where the Mauryan throne room of Ashoka's palace was discovered, to supporting Mahatma Gandhi's early work among the Indian community in South Africa. He provided funds so that the University of London could investigate the causes of poverty and how to eradicate it. In 1912, he offered an annual stipend of £1400 to study the causes of destitution and potential suggestions for relief over a three-year period. This stipend was awarded through 1931. Before Sir Ratan died in 1918, he asked that his wealth be used to support education, health care, rural communities and art and culture via the Sir Ratan Tata Trust.

Dorab registered the Sir Dorabji Tata Trust shortly before his death, and bequeathed nearly all his wealth to it, including his holdings in Tata Sons, his property, twenty-one pieces of his late wife's jewellery (which included the famed Jubilee Diamond), as well as his own personal accessories. At the time, the value of the assets was approximately $10 million. Today, the figure would be closer to $500 million.

The Sir Dorabji Tata Trust dedicated much of its support to six national institutions, including the Tata Institute of Social Sciences, the Tata Memorial Centre for Cancer Research and Treatment, the Tata Institute of Fundamental Research, the National Centre for the Performing Arts, the National Institute of Advanced Studies, and the Sir Dorabji Tata Centre for Research in Tropical Diseases. All of these were established after Dorab's death, but they reflect his intentions for his legacy.

When his wife, Lady Meherbai, died of leukaemia in 1931, at the age of fifty, Dorab started two trusts in her memory: the Lady Meherbai D. Tata Education Trust and the Lady Tata Memorial Trust. The education trust supports advanced education for women, and the memorial trust funds important, and often groundbreaking, research into leukaemia and other diseases. Some of the research recently conducted under the trust auspices qualified for the Nobel Prize.

The J.R.D. Tata Trust, which JRD established in 1944, supports education, research and community development. It grants scholarships, provides disaster relief and funds social welfare projects.

Like businesses that have expanded and are in need of consolidation, the Tata trusts have now been expanded and combined as the Sir Dorabji Tata Trust and Allied Trusts. The Allied Trusts are smaller and include the Tata Social Welfare Trust, the R.D. Tata Trust, the Tata Education Trust, the J.R.D. Tata Trust, the J.R.D. Tata and Thelma Tata Trust, the Jamsetji Tata Trust, the J.N. Tata Endowment, the Lady Meherbai Tata Memorial Trust, and the Lady Meherbai Tata Education Trust. The Sir Dorabji Tata Trust and the Allied Trusts provide financial support to more than 600 non-governmental organizations in six social development sectors: natural resource management and livelihoods; urban poverty and livelihoods; education; health; civil society, governance, human rights; and media, art and culture. Among the Tata trusts, the Sir Ratan Tata Trust is the other major player, alongside the Sir Dorabji Tata Trust and Allied Trusts.

Catalysts for Change

All of the Tata trusts work to apply their financial resources to foster significant change in India, for the benefit of its people. Whether investing in education reform, providing the means for India's top scholars to study abroad, dedicating a sizeable sum to the eradication of disease, or funding programmes to aid children with special needs, the Tata trusts are serious about their work. They don't simply throw money at a problem, but invest it wisely, targeting areas where it is possible to make a positive difference. A portion of each trust's disbursements is also set aside for individual grants. For example, one grant of 125 rupees was given to an older man who needed new glasses and could not afford them. Did that grant change the country? No, but for that man, it meant the difference between light and darkness. This approach reflects Parsi religious doctrine, which holds that changing the life of even one other person for the better means that your life has purpose.

What is perhaps most remarkable about the Tata trusts is their adaptability. Like many entrepreneurial organizations, these massive trusts change to meet the changing needs of society. Just as Tata Sons remains flexible and nimble with respect to the management of its many business units, so, too, the trusts are agile and structured to best serve the most important or pressing needs.

Part of the adaptability of the trusts is due to their having evolved from a donor-dependent model to one of partnerships and joint ventures with other organizations. It was Ratan Tata who said: 'Philanthropic institutions in India still believe they're charitable and therefore must operate on a shoestring, [and] that creating an organization is almost a luxury. This needs to change. They have to recognize that a non-profit has as much responsibility for being professionally run as a corporate body.'[1] Hence the introduction of business processes and strategies for growth.

JRD may have said it best when he explained the impact Jamsetji Tata's family had on all of India through their trusts: 'The wealth gathered by Jamsetji Tata and his sons in half a century of industrial pioneering formed but a minute fraction of the amount by which they enriched the nation. The whole of that wealth is held in trust for the people and used exclusively for their benefit. The cycle is thus complete. What came from the people has gone back to the people many times over.'[2]

---

[1] Prince Thomas, 'How Ratan Tata is gearing up for his transition in December', *Forbes India*, Blogs/Business & Strategy, 3 August 2012; available online at: http://forbesindia.com/blog/business-strategy/how-ratan-tata-is-gearing-up-for-his-transition-in-december/.
[2] 'Giving back to the people'; available online at: http://www.tata.com/aboutus/articlesinside/xigCYABhsUM=/TLYVr3YPkMU.

NINE

THE IMPORTANCE OF PASSION

Entrepreneurs who are passionate about a Big Idea enjoy much greater odds of success than would-be business owners who are just in it for the money. Jamsetji Tata was never interested in making money for money's sake. His eyes were always on the good that money could do. But he was deeply interested in textiles, hydroelectricity and education. These, in fact, were among his driving passions.

A recent American Express survey of 600 business owners found that entrepreneurs motivated by their passion were much more likely to have experienced higher revenue growth during the past three years. The most successful entrepreneurs leverage what they are interested in or excited about, whether it is a hobby or a personal interest, to create a business that serves like-minded customers. Jamsetji Tata, founder of Tata Sons, is the perfect example of a passionate entrepreneur—albeit not in the obvious or traditional sense.

Jamsetji did not have a hobby or activity he was obsessed with—in contrast to JRD, who was obsessed with airplanes, or sports fanatic Dorab. He was, however, intensely passionate about his personal mission to industrialize his country. He recognized that he had the opportunity to help modernize India and thereby improve the lot of the less fortunate among his fellow countrymen. And so he founded a company based on what he knew best—textiles—and he worked to make that company the very best it could be, for excellence was another of Jamsetji's passions—in particular, excellence in the service of others. It was an unstoppable combination, and Jamsetji passed it down to subsequent Tata company leaders. They, of course, also understood that Tata Sons was blessed with the opportunity to truly and profoundly change India.

Passionate about Altruism

Steve Jobs was passionate about creativity and innovation, a combination he parlayed into Apple, which has designed revolutionary products. Mary Kay Ash, founder of Mary Kay Cosmetics, was passionate about cosmetics as a means of making women feel good about themselves. George Eastman, consumed with photography from a very young age, founded Eastman Kodak Company. Jamsetji Tata was also passionate, but his passion stemmed from a deep desire to change his part of the world. It was his life's mission.

Unlike most entrepreneurs, Jamsetji started a business as a way to make other things possible, not because he was particularly inspired by cotton or textiles. He was passionate about excellence, however, which he applied to every aspect of his life. It was a passion that drove him to build the best business possible, providing the best care and opportunities for employees and generating the most revenue possible—ultimately to benefit the surrounding community. The same level of passion was also evident in J.R.D. Tata, who found a way to merge his love of flying with his family's growing enterprise.

Founding an airline that provided a mail service and then a passenger service connected India in a way that had not been possible before. His passion fuelled a new type of travel as well as the expansion of the Tata empire.

'Ratan Tata is passionate about what he believes in,' Tata Sons executive director R. Gopalakrishnan says. Where previous leaders had outside interests, Ratan was more focused on doing what is best for the company. He was passionate about his work, reliant on his capable staff, and known for his decisiveness. According to his staff, few of his decisions ever required more than forty-eight hours to make.

Cyrus Mistry is also passionate and has begun making hard decisions about how to improve performance at some of the Tata units.

An Air of Excitement

Entrepreneurs who are passionate about what they invest their time in stand out. Their enthusiasm for their work is evident in how they walk, how they talk, the expressions they use, and how engaged they are with others. Their enthusiasm is contagious, even when they are discussing subjects unrelated to their business. They have about them an air of confidence and positive energy.

It is clear that the leaders of Tata were passionate about their work—not how they made money, but how they used the money they made to serve those around them. Stories continue to circulate about how Jamsetji Tata approached experts to ask for their help in bringing about major changes in India. One such anecdote involves Charles Page Perin, an American metallurgical engineer tapped by Jamsetji to help build a steel plant in India. In describing their first meeting, Perin recalled, 'I was poring over some accounts in the office when the door opened and a stranger in a strange garb entered. He walked in, leaned over my desk and looked at me fully a minute in silence. Finally, he said in a deep voice, "Are you Charles Page Perin?" I said, "Yes." He stared at me again silently for a long time, and then slowly he said, "I believe I have found the man I have been looking for. I want you to come to India with me, to find suitable iron ore and coking coal and the necessary fluxes. Mr Kennedy will build the steel plant wherever you advise and I will foot the bill. Will you come to India with me?"

'I was dumbfounded, naturally,' Perin admits. 'But you don't know what character and force radiated from Tata's face. And kindliness, too. "Well," I said, "yes, I'd go." And I did.'[1]

Jamsetji had that effect on people. His passion for his life's work radiated from him, drawing others to him in support of his work. Much the same can be said of the Tata leaders who succeeded him. Their personal commitment to their work attracted others who supported their altruism and philanthropy. Who, after all, could argue with a man who wanted only what was best for his nation and its people?

---

[1] R.M. Lala, *Beyond the Last Blue Mountain: A Life of J.R.D. Tata* (New Delhi: Penguin Portfolio, 1993), p. 44.

TEN

THE VALUE OF INDEPENDENCE

Despite leading dozens of businesses, management at Tata has historically felt no need to micromanage the heads of each business unit. Confident in their personnel choices, chairmen in the past have allowed individual business units and leaders to operate as they saw fit. The result has been unprecedented personal commitment to the business.

Western corporations have a preference for consolidation, for lumping business units and divisions together under one banner to make it clear as to who is in charge. It's a control issue, really. In many cases, the businesses are disparate and unrelated, but they are nevertheless force-fitted into the corporate hierarchy. Decision-making comes from above and trickles down to the various companies, whether a particular direction and rationale truly make sense for all or not. Often, it does not.

Anxious to make sure everyone understands who really has the upper hand, CEOs traditionally create direct-reporting relationships and matrices, all of which are designed to reduce independence. Tata Sons does precisely the opposite.

Maybe it's the expectation of excellence, or the knowledge that everyone is working for the greater good, but there is far less micromanagement at Tata than in virtually any other major corporate enterprise. Independence is built into the Tata DNA. From the company's inception, Tata Sons has insisted on hiring only the best leaders, the best employees, using the best equipment, and creating the best work environments.

The Tata Sons chairman gives business units all the support and guidance they need concerning organization-wide goals. How that goal is to be reached, however, is largely left to the judgement of individual company CEOs. Separate and distinct from Tata Sons, these leaders are nevertheless part of the extended family.

Avoiding Conflicts of Interest

Independence is not just an ethos and a creative way of doing business. It also serves to avoid even the appearance of conflict-of-interest. As Tata has grown and expanded into nearly every industry sector on the planet, avoiding conflict-of-interest situations has become ever more challenging. If the conglomerated companies were all managed by a single leader, there would be no way of avoiding conflicts. Whatever else it does, the concept of independence keeps the operating companies at arm's length from Tata Sons. By operating with glass walls between them, Tata's many businesses can see what the others are doing and learn from them, without being directly involved in them. This essential independence keeps the business units separate, distinct, and largely free of conflicts.

Protective walls are especially important when one Tata company is pursuing a client that competes with a sister Tata company. Such situations are becoming more common as Tata continues to expand. Some of the same reasoning applies to Tata's current joint ventures with Singapore Airlines and Air Asia. Tata is invested in both airlines, but it keeps them separate to avoid any potential for conflict—even though there should be none, say industry experts, because the two ventures are pursuing very different markets. Singapore Airlines targets premium clientele, whereas Air Asia aims to serve the economy-minded. There is ample room for both, and as long as they do operate independently, Tata's airline partners should have no qualms. As for any fear of monopoly, the companies are not only separate and distinct, they even compete in some instances.

With regard to its policy on acquisitions, Tata uses a light touch when it comes to integrating new companies into the fold. Ratan Tata described the group's approach to its acquisition of South Korea's Daewoo Commercial Vehicle Company in 2004 thus: 'Tata Motors will operate Daewoo as a Korean company in Korea, managed by Koreans, but it will work as part of a global alliance with its Indian counterpart.'[1] Put another way, Daewoo would continue to operate separately, independently, under an India-based parent company.

Becoming a Global Powerhouse

From its start in the late 1800s to the end of the 1900s, Tata Sons was focused narrowly on the Indian market. It was a huge market in itself, and for a hundred years, it provided ample opportunity for the corporation's growth. However, under Ratan Tata's leadership, starting in the late 1990s, Tata Sons began to look beyond India's borders. In the mid-2000s, the company announced that it had identified eight 'priority' countries expected to provide the greatest opportunities for Tata's growth: the US, the UK, Singapore, South Africa, the United Arab Emirates, South Korea, China and Bangladesh.

At the same time, as Tata expanded globally, it also focused on a smaller set of industries within the global

---

[1] R.M. Srivastava and Shubhra Verma, *Strategic Management: Concepts, Skills and Practices* (New Delhi: PHI Learning Private Limited, 2012), p. 299.

marketplace. Tata Sons invested more of its resources in seven specific sectors which have been responsible for generating much of the company's revenues since 2000: materials, energy, consumer products, telecom, IT services, chemicals and engineering. By acquiring larger stakes in companies within these seven sectors, Tata tried to consolidate its efforts without actually consolidating the companies themselves. It's a tricky balance, which Tata has been managing masterfully.

A Question of Ethics

The fact that Tata Sons holds an ownership stake in companies in virtually every industry might be of concern if we were talking about any other company but Tata. The danger of internal information-sharing certainly exists and, were the company any other, there would be resistance to doing business with some Tata units. Competitors would very likely be worried about sharing inside information with one division of Tata, which could be communicated to its Tata-owned competitor. But because Tata takes great care to ensure that no information is shared and its corporate culture forbids such unethical behaviour, Tata companies simply do not collude, trade secrets or risk any action that would tarnish the Tata reputation.

Outsiders have faith that no Tata company would act in any way that puts in jeopardy a nearly 150-year reputation for ethics and excellence. They know that the culture of ethics that started with Jamsetji continues today as the driving force throughout Tata. Doing what is right is more important than doing what is profitable or advantageous. Any action that puts Tata's integrity in question is unacceptable and will not be tolerated. Because that message is so clear, competitors rarely worry that Tata will take advantage of them, nor do potential clients worry that they will be put at a disadvantage by hiring a Tata division.

Thanks to its ethical reputation and the total absence of incidents in which insider information was shared, TCS can work on automotive consulting contracts even though its parent company also owns automotive manufacturers. Likewise, TCS can advise consumer packaged goods companies, while Tata Sons owns such brands as Tetley Tea. The guarantee of ethics would hold even if Tata companies operated as one huge corporation. But the ethics are combined with the unique structure of Tata Sons, in which each business is independent from the others. Morally and structurally, Tata is designed to be conflict-free.

ELEVEN

THE PILLARS OF ETHICS AND GOVERNANCE

Many corporations give lip service to words like 'ethics' and 'governance'; Tata has built a business around the principles. Striving to be ethical in all aspects of its business has earned Tata goodwill and respect that carry over to its brand identity.

Tata Sons has flourished for more than 140 years because of its extremely high standards of performance. However, unlike virtually every other company, it does not put financial performance first. Because one of its main drivers is to fund charitable work, the Tata group of companies is much more concerned about honesty and integrity and the common good than it is about generating sales. Perhaps because of its broader social mission, ethics and governance reign supreme at Tata Sons. The Tata shareholders know that they could probably get a slightly higher return on their investment if they invested in a company that did not make such a large pledge to charitable causes, but they know that their money is in safer hands at Tata.

From the outset, Jamsetji Tata made clear what he expected of those working with him. He wanted their best efforts, of course, and he also wanted ethical behaviour. Today, the company has formalized these standards, and employees, partners, and suppliers are all required to abide by them. And therein lies one of the biggest differences between Tata and just about every other organization. Unlike Western corporations that invest months in drafting formal codes of conduct that can be immediately filed away and ignored, Tata expects all those associated with the business to live up to them. Those who fail to are invited to work elsewhere.

With ethical behaviour at the fore, the company has carefully defined the conduct that is considered acceptable in pursuing its corporate goals. This is the essence of its corporate governance: a set of processes that ensure the company is doing what is best for all of its stakeholders. Any activity that damages its reputation is not tolerated, and the firm places great importance on integrity, understanding, excellence, unity and responsibility. Unscrupulous individuals need not apply.

The Tata Code of Conduct

Tata Sons attracts ethical employees because it has always been vocal about its ethical standards and its expectations of ethicality from its employees. Formally committed to paper in 1998, the TCoC expresses the company's values in a straightforward way that makes crystal clear what is expected of anyone associated with the company (see Appendix B). In addition to defining the company's value system, the code lays out what honourable behaviour is and specifies that employees, partners, independent contractors, consultants and suppliers be expected to adhere to those standards.

Doing what is right was always the company's litmus

test, even as it relates to taxes. Ratan once told a story about JRD's clear sense of right and wrong. While most business owners take great pains to reduce taxes, JRD was in the minority. His motto was tax compliance, not tax avoidance, let alone tax evasion. At one point, a senior Tata executive found an opportunity to save some money on taxes. The chairman of the company insisted that he present his thinking to JRD before the chairman would approve it. The executive explained the tax-saving strategy and concluded with: 'It is not illegal.'

'Not illegal, yes,' JRD responded softly. 'But is it right?'

The tax consultant who retells the story, Dinesh Vyas, says that no one had ever asked him that question. Vyas later wrote: 'JRD would have been the most ardent supporter of the view expressed by Lord Denning: "The avoidance of tax may be lawful, but it is not yet a virtue."'[1]

---

[1] R.M. Lala, 'The business ethics of J.R.D. Tata', *The Hindu*, 29 July 2004; available online at: http://www.hindu.com/2004/07/29/stories/2004072905951200.htm.

More recently, I personally witnessed a commitment to ethics that surprised me, but on reflection it should not have. My company had been hired to help find an executive for TCS. We identified a candidate for a C-level position who was well qualified for the role. His experience matched up perfectly with what TCS needed. The only problem was that he had signed a non-compete clause with his last employer, and it was still in effect. He had promised not to work in the same industry for a period of twelve months, but now he wanted to work at TCS. In practice, non-competes are rarely enforceable. In the US, no one takes them seriously because they are so easily dismissed. But Tata did.

TCS really wanted to hire this candidate, so they made him an offer. However, that offer was contingent on his getting a signed waiver from his current employer releasing him from the non-compete agreement. TCS said, in essence: 'Yes, we know they can't enforce it, but we want them to let you out of it before we hire you.' As it happened, he couldn't get the waiver, and so TCS did not hire him.

Where most American companies think nothing of overlooking or contesting non-compete agreements,

Tata expected this candidate to be a man of his word. This is how Tata always does business. The company's commitment to doing what is right is more important than doing what is expedient or profitable. This goes to the core of the TCoC.

Strong Corporate Governance

You might think that within a company consisting of more than 130 operating business units, providing a single set of standards of behaviour would be quite impossible. To make this assumption about Tata Sons would grossly underestimate the firm. Adherence to high standards of conduct actually goes deeper than the Brand Equity and Business Promotion Agreement and the TCoC. These documents are written on paper, but the firm's true corporate governance needs no memorandum. It is ingrained in the company's way of thinking, and it unerringly guides the behaviour of all Tata stakeholders. The unwritten code is very simple. Asking and answering the question, 'Is this the right thing to do for all involved?' is its sum and substance.

Corporate governance, or the way in which Tata

Sons manages its many operating divisions, is dictated by the pervasive theme of service to others. Whereas many boards of directors are primarily concerned with executive pay increases and evading responsibility for wrongdoing, the Tata board is deeply concerned with living up to the grand expectations that its stakeholders have for the company and its products. The question, 'Is this the right thing to do?' is applied to nearly every situation, whether it affects employees, customers, suppliers, stakeholders, local residents or others. As a concomitant principle, money earned by the company must be used for the common good.

A Caring Corporate Culture

Most for-profit businesses view workers as assets to be leveraged. In other words, employees exist to serve their employers. Jamsetji Tata, however, took the opposite view. As he saw it, business and industry were meant to serve humankind. As he explained in his speech at the 1895 opening of an addition to Empress Mills, 'We do not claim to be more unselfish, more generous and more philanthropic than other people. But we think we started on sound and straightforward business principles, considering the interests of the shareholders our own, and the health and welfare of the employees the sure foundation of our prosperity.'[2] These words encapsulate Jamsetji's mission, which remains the company's mission today. Tata Sons is in business to care for others. By setting a positive example for those others, the company inspires others to make a difference, each in their own way.

And they have. Tata employees have initiated community service programmes, gathered donations, and pitched in to aid others, all in an effort to follow in Jamsetji's footsteps. With Jamsetji as a role model, employees at every level look for ways in which they, too, can make a difference. Tata leaders are and always have been deeply concerned for the greater good.

They take responsibility for supporting whole communities when Tata plants are built. They employ local residents, provide education and raise the standard of living for everyone in the area.

---

[2] 'The quotable Jamsetji Tata', March 2008; available online at: http://www.tata.com/aboutus/articlesinside/1U2QamAhqtA=/TLYVr3YPkMU=.

They employ workers with special needs whenever possible. Titan set a record for employing the highest percentage of disabled people in any factory in India—4.4 per cent. The figure was higher than the government-recommended 3.5 per cent, and much higher than the typical disabled employment rate, which, at the time, was below 1 per cent.

Employees feel a responsibility to care for others. When natural disasters strike, it is not uncommon for workers at Tata Steel and Telco to offer to donate a day's wages to those affected. For its part, Tata frequently matches the amount donated or contributes above and beyond what is collected.

Secret of Success

Perhaps because the company's positive contributions to society are so visible, it is ultra-protective of its public persona. Even the mere appearance of impropriety is avoided at all costs, for fear that it will damage the deep trust the company has established with its stakeholders. Invariably, operating as an ethical business, overseen by a board of directors whose vision is perfectly aligned with that of the late Jamsetji Tata, Tata Sons remains successful by refusing to compromise the original corporate vision.

TWELVE

THE IMPORTANCE OF SERVANT LEADERSHIP

While the concept of servant leadership is much talked about, its implementation is all too rare in Western business. It is, however, at the core of Tata Sons—and has been since the beginning. Instead of starting a business to serve himself or his family, Jamsetji Tata built a business that—by design—existed to serve. This is the essence of servant leadership: leading your enterprise in the service of others, which encompasses employees, members of the larger community, customers, partners, shareholders and the society at large.

The question most Western businesses ask is: 'How can we make the most money?' This question is at their core, and that, in turn, impacts every facet of the organization, from who is hired, where facilities are located, operational principles, priorities and ethics. Truthfully, this is the antithesis of the businesses the Tatas have always endeavoured to run. At Tata, servant leadership is more than a management principle or strategy. It is a way of life and a way of viewing the world. 'What can we do for others?' is the central question that drives the business. Being relentlessly other-focused ensures a sustainable organization.

Caring for Employees

Your employees treat your customers the way you treat your employees. It is a simple maxim—a kind of extension of the golden rule, and just as true. To enable employees to contribute to the greatest extent possible, the employer must discover what they need. It may be better equipment, more instruction, more breaks during the day or simply more sunlight.

Jamsetji understood this. He took the time and spent the money to ensure that workers in his textile mills had adequate fresh air—a vital commodity that few, if any, mill owners ever considered—as well as reasonable working hours. Corporate leaders who take the time to discover their employees' needs can then empower them to be more productive, more engaged, more loyal, and generally happier. Believe it or not, happiness does matter, on or off the job. Jamsetji Tata and those who followed him understood this.

Despite its vast and growing size, Tata takes a profound and genuinely benevolent interest in each and every one of its employees. And those workers feel it. No wonder that employee attrition at TCS is 12.8 per cent (versus 15.4 per cent for its closest competitor, Infosys). Why do people stay with Tata? A big part of the reason is loyalty—two-way loyalty, which is the only true form of loyalty—and devotion, which is also mutual between employee and employer. Employees appreciate the care and concern management shows them. One result is longevity. The other is a level of productivity considerably higher than that of average workers.

Although TCS employs over 300,000 workers, 93 per cent from India, each individual is made to feel special and important—a cherished member of the Tata family. One employee reported that upon notifying his manager that his father had fallen ill, he was immediately offered, without even asking, a month's leave, and all of his insurance paperwork was expedited.

Tata invests in its employees. In addition to competitive salaries, TCS benefits include an insurance package that is one of the best, not only in India, but in the industry in general. The company also offers a strong employee assistance programme, and devotes time and effort to bring together employees and their families for local events. Such benefits and demonstrations of caring have earned TCS recognition (in a *Business Today*–Indicus Analytics annual survey) as India's best company to work for.

Relations of Synergy

Although many large business organizations have been flattening out, hierarchies in one form or another still prevail. Senior management is at the top, workers at the bottom. Ultimately, the topmost executives make all the decisions about how the company will be run. Once made, the decisions trickle down to the various levels of workers, who are expected to carry out management's directives. If there is doubt or disagreement, subordinates rarely get a vote.

Contrast this with the servant-leader model, in which relationships between leaders and employees are far more synergistic. Top, bottom or middle, everyone agrees on working towards the same goal that benefits all.

There is discussion and collaboration to create the best tactic for achieving each objective on the way towards the common goal. Senior managers assume responsibility—not for credit and commendation, but for the sake of ensuring that workers have everything they need to achieve the goals all have bought into. Senior managers serve the workers. It's the traditional corporate hierarchy turned upside down.

Frugality as a Virtue

While Tata Sons continues to grow and thrive as an enterprise, the family members who are shareholders do not aim narrowly to profit from its success. Instead of siphoning off profits, Tata leaders have always been careful about the benefits they have received from their association with the company. They do not live lavishly, nor make extravagant displays of wealth with fancy cars or dress or purchases. They see money not as an end, but as a means to an end—improving the lives of the people of India.

I was in India recently and Tata sent a car to pick me up for a meeting. On the way there, my driver exclaimed: 'Look, there is Mr Tata!' Sure enough, Ratan's car had pulled up right beside mine at the traffic lights. The car he was being driven in was a Tata Indica, one of the smallest cars in the Tata Motors range, and half the size of the one they had sent to pick me up. Unfortunately, he pulled away before I could get a photograph or else it would have been included in the book.

They are, to use an old-fashioned word, frugal. Frugality, recognizing the value of all resources so that you do not squander them, is a key element of the servant-leader philosophy the Tata family lives by and by which they run the companies. No money goes to waste. It is invested in the companies' stakeholders to enable the continued growth of the business, which then permits continued—and expanded—reinvestment in the community and a better return for the shareholders.

THIRTEEN

WHAT WOULD JAMSETJI DO IF HE WERE RUNNING TATA TODAY?

New Tata Group chairman, Cyrus Mistry, has some challenging decisions to make. Just as opportunities for greatness stretched out before Jamsetji Tata nearly a century and a half ago, they are there the same way for Cyrus. This is the start of a new era for Tata, and there are a vast number of choices to be made about where the company will focus its resources to do the most good, and reward investors, customers and employees. Cyrus has an opportunity to make his mark by guiding the company to even greater accomplishments.

Cyrus assumed the chairman's role in 2012, when he was just forty-five, after Ratan Tata's retirement. He is the first person outside of the Tata family to become chairman. While the Mistry family has a vested financial interest in the continued success of the company, both families partake in Parsi values, especially the mission to give back and improve the lives of others.

There is a lot of weight on this young man's shoulders, and he is now responsible for the largest company in India and one of the biggest in the world. To put Tata in perspective, consider that the largest family business in the United States is Walmart, with more than $400 billion in sales. Tata is not all that far behind, with earnings of more than $100 billion.

Cyrus is known for being decisive, a trait that surely contributed to his success, along with his brother, in turning around group infrastructure company Afcons, as well as expanding Shapoorji Pallonji. His unassuming style and ability to get along with everyone are possibly among the main reasons he was selected to lead Tata.

Confronted with questions about where to go next and how to get there, many companies look back in order to see ahead. They reflect on their roots and the paths that took them to their current situation. What values have helped shape the business? What strategies have proven most effective? How can more profit be obtained? These are the questions typically asked. Tata, naturally, is different. Even more important than the company's business goals are its social initiatives. Management routinely asks itself, 'How can Tata best aid India?' This, in turn, begs the question: 'Where should Cyrus turn his attention?'

For an answer, we can do no better than to ask Jamsetji Tata, the man whose foresight and concern for India created an entirely new business model. No matter that Jamsetji died in 1904, we know what he did, what he said, what he believed, and why. We understand the spiritual, philosophical and historical contexts in which Jamsetji's decisions were made. We can extrapolate from the nineteenth century into the twenty-first and draw some conclusions about what Jamsetji would do if he were Cyrus Pallonji Mistry.

Education

I have no doubt that Jamsetji would today focus, first and foremost, on education. He believed that only through education could the impoverished and disadvantaged change their fate. He donated a vast amount of his personal wealth to establish institutes of higher learning as well as academic scholarships, all with the intention of raising the level of education nationwide.

Jamsetji clearly saw the connection between education and wealth, and he wanted every Indian to be given the opportunity to work and earn a good living. This was possible only through learning. While today—thanks to Jamsetji's massive endowment—India has some of the best science and research universities in the world, the number of Indian students who want to attend them is overwhelming and the available resources so limited in proportion that entrance requirements for the best schools are very nearly impossible to meet. A college in Delhi University, for example, required minimum test scores of 100 per cent in 2013. An applicant who fell short of numerical perfection was not even considered.

Without intervention, the chasm between educational supply and demand will only get deeper and wider. Half of India's 1.2-billion-strong population is under twenty-five. Many among this huge group dream of a college education, but there simply isn't enough space in Indian colleges and universities. Some, therefore, go abroad for their studies, but not everyone can afford to do so—and fewer still can foot the bill for an Ivy League education or its equivalent.

By investing in the construction and staffing of new institutes of higher learning in India, Cyrus can do what Jamsetji would surely have done: act to close the gap between supply and demand. But, as an innovator, Jamsetji, were he among us, would also look beyond brick and mortar. The future of education is in Massive Open Online Courses (or MOOCs). MOOCs will do for education what iTunes did for music, make education available to the masses at a fraction of the brick-and-mortar cost. MOOCs will also bridge the gap between what universities produce and what businesses need, reducing the time lag from seven years to one.

They will allow Tata, for example, to train and educate its huge workforce. Tata being Tata, the company will doubtless leverage its MOOC system throughout India, indeed, the world, and not just within the Tata network of companies.

Health Care

Jamsetji understood that if you don't have health, you don't have wealth. Providing preventive care through in-house doctors and nurses at Tata companies has helped improve the overall health of employees, the vast majority of whom are also residents of the communities in which Tata offices and plants are located. Still, many who do not work for Tata have inadequate health care.

While India's universal health-care system is far better today than it was 140 years ago, challenges persist. In the poorest communities, where residents cannot afford even basic treatment, diseases long ago eradicated in other parts of the world continue to afflict them. When families have no food or clothing, health care becomes an unaffordable luxury. The lack of affordability is compounded by a shortage of doctors, especially in rural areas. India has 0.6 physicians per 1000 residents—and most of this small number practise in the cities. Faced with rising demand for health-care services, Jamsetji would surely invest in educating more doctors and also in extending medical outreach to provide services to those in need in more remote parts of the country.

Pakistan

While conflict with other countries was not a major issue during Jamsetji's lifetime, it is certainly a concern in Cyrus Mistry's world. Nuclear-armed Pakistan, India's neighbour, is a continual threat.

What would Jamsetji do about it if he were present to guide Tata? He would invest in Pakistan. He understood that economic investments solve a lot of problems, and creating a more dependent economic relationship between India and Pakistan could override and alleviate a lot of animosity, thereby reducing military tensions.

Energy

One of Jamsetji's true passions was energy, a sector he approached in the hope of one day providing hydroelectric power to India. Although it did not happen in his lifetime, it did ultimately happen, and the widespread availability of electricity created new opportunities for growth and expansion in the subcontinent.

Today, the challenge of providing adequate power throughout India remains, but the issue is now centred on the use of nuclear energy. Would Jamsetji favour using nuclear technology in order to provide electricity? I think he would have preferred that we had not discovered nuclear energy. However, let us assume that he understood the risks, even though he had not lived through Hiroshima and Nagasaki or, more to the point, Three Mile Island, Chernobyl and Fukushima. I believe that being a realist, he would understand that we cannot put the nuclear genie back into the bottle. On that basis, and by understanding and accepting that with great rewards come great risks, Jamsetji would likely have appreciated that the rewards of nuclear power, given India's great need, outweigh the risks.

Poverty

Jamsetji was a forward thinker who constantly sought solutions to improve living conditions across India. Even today, of course, poverty continues to ravage parts of India. The challenge, now as then, is how to introduce improvements that do not threaten a community's way of life. Being the strong facilitator that he was, Jamsetji would probably seek to work with the Arab and Islamic communities to learn how they maintain their cultural identities while adopting modern improvements.

Going Truly Global with Tata's Message

I believe that Jamsetji, having realized the success of the Tata model, would seek to expand the philanthropic initiatives globally and would be fully supportive of initiatives such as the Tata Engage programme, so that the philanthropic reach of the Tata ideals can touch every country in the world. Can you imagine the impact it would have on the world if other major companies followed suit? The Tata Engage initiative is a programme that encourages Tata employees to donate half a day a year to any charity in the country they are working in—and they receive full pay whilst doing so.

Pope Francis has spoken out against global poverty, explaining that the capitalist trickle-down economic model is not working, for the reasons I outlined in the beginning of this book.

Maybe governments around the world should examine the Tata model. There is a way for capitalism and socialism to work together in harmony. Maybe that way is the Tata model.

What Is to Come?

What Cyrus himself decides to focus on will depend on his passions and interests, and where he sees the greatest need. We believe that at least some of the areas outlined above will capture his imagination and move his will. Personally, I hope that he will visit my homeland and recognize that Ireland would be a perfect partner to launch a MOOC-based platform of education with. The goal? To revolutionize the Indian education system in India and give Tata companies an unassailable advantage over their competitors in terms of knowledge transfer, dramatically improving the level of education in India by extending it to the lowest levels of society. Ireland could provide India with a perfect springboard into Europe and a direct connection with the hundreds of major American companies based in the country. It would also re-establish Ireland as the land of saints and scholars.

APPENDIX A

TATA BUSINESS SECTORS AND COMPANIES

The depth and breadth of Tata Sons' holdings is truly impressive, surpassing that of any global conglomerate now in existence. Other firms that formerly held vast holdings in a wide range of industries have long since consolidated, selling off non-core businesses in order to focus on slim vertical markets. Tata went another route. Instead of focusing more acutely, the executive team elected to expand and diversify. The result is a current portfolio of more than 130 companies in industries ranging from consumer products to automotive to energy, retail, insurance, aviation and more.

The top units include some of the world's leading brand names: companies like TCS, which recently surpassed Accenture in market cap, and Tata Steel, the twelfth-largest steel-producing company in the world in 2012, with manufacturing operations in twenty-six countries. Tata Global Beverages is the umbrella brand for consumer products such as Tetley Tea, the second-largest tea manufacturer and distributor in the world, and Eight O'Clock Coffee, another global powerhouse. The Indian Hotels Company oversees the Taj Hotels chain, the pre-eminent luxury hotel chain in India, as well as other global hotel chains. Tata Motors includes acquired brands, such as Jaguar and Land Rover, as well as its own pioneering car models, including the Nano.

Through in-house innovation and savvy acquisitions, Tata now owns and manages companies in nearly every industry on the planet. The revenue generated supports the work of the Tata trusts, which own a 66 per cent stake in the conglomerate.

The following is a list of renowned Tata companies.[1]

Chemicals

- Advinus Therapeutics
- Rallis India
- Tata Chemicals
- Tata Chemicals Europe
- Tata Chemical Magadi
- Tata Chemicals North America
- Tata Pigments

Consumer products

- Casa Décor
- Infiniti Retail
- Landmark
- Tata Ceramics
- Tata Global Beverages
- Titan Company
- Trent
- Westland

---

[1] This list is current as of 30 June 2014.

Energy

- Powerlinks Transmission
- Tata Petrodyne
- Tata Power
- Tata Power Delhi Distribution
- Tata Power Solar Systems
- Tata Power Trading

Engineering products and services

- TAL Manufacturing Solutions
- TAS-AGT Systems
- Tata Advanced Systems
- Tata Consulting Engineers
- Tata Industrial Services
- Tata Projects
- TRF
- Voltas
- Jaguar Land Rover
- Tata AutoComp Systems
- Tata Cummins
- Tata Daewoo Commercial Vehicle Company
- Tata Hitachi Construction Machinery

- Tata Motors
- Tata Motors European Technical Centre

Materials

- Hooghly Met Coke and Power Company
- Indian Steel and Wire Products
- JAMIPOL
- mjunction services
- NatSteel Holdings
- Tata BlueScope Steel
- Tata Metaliks
- Tata NYK
- Tata Sponge Iron
- Tata Steel
- Tata Steel Europe
- Tata Steel KZN
- Tata Steel Processing and Distribution
- Tata Steel Thailand
- Tayo Rolls
- The Tinplate Company of India
- TM International Logistics
- TRL Krosaki Refractors
- Tata Advanced Materials

Services

- Drive India Enterprise Solutions
- Indian Hotels
- Jamshedpur Utilities and Services Company
- Roots Corporation
- Taj Air
- Tata Housing Development Company
- Tata Reality and Infrastructure
- e-nxt Financials
- Tata AIA Life Insurance
- Tata AIG General Insurance
- Tata Asset Management
- Tata Capital
- Tata Investment Corporation
- Associated Building Company
- Tata AG
- Tata International
- Tata International AG
- Tata Limited
- Tata Quality Management Services
- Tata Services
- Tata Strategic Management Group
- TKM Global Logistics

- Tata Africa Holding
- Tata Sons
- Tata Industries

Information technology and communications

- CMC
- Nelito Systems
- Tata Business Support Services
- TCS
- Tata Elxsi
- Tata Interactive Systems
- Tata Technologies
- Nelco
- Tata Communications
- Tata Sky
- Tata Teleservices
- Tata Teleservices (Maharashtra)
- Tatanet

THE TATA CODE OF CONDUCT

Foreword

The Tata Code of Conduct is a set of principles that guide and govern the conduct of Tata companies and their employees in all matters relating to business. First elucidated in 1998, the Code lays down the ethical standards that Tata employees have to observe in their professional lives, and it defines the value system at the heart of the Tata Group and its many business entities.

The Code is a dynamic document that reinforces the Tata canon of honourable behaviour in business. While it has remained unaltered at its core, the Code has been modified down the years to keep it in step with changing regulatory norms in the different parts of the world that Tata companies now do business. These modifications have reinforced the Code, and enable it to reflect the diverse business, cultural and other factors that have a bearing on the health of the Tata brand.

If all of us, in our professional and personal capacities, can internalize the beliefs enshrined in the Tata Code of Conduct, the Tata Group's legacy and its future will remain in good hands.

C.P. Mistry
Group Chairman

National interest

The Tata Group is committed to benefit the economic development of the countries in which it operates. No Tata company shall undertake any project or activity to the detriment of the wider interests of the communities in which it operates.

A Tata company's management practices and business conduct shall benefit the country, localities and communities in which it operates, to the extent possible and affordable, and shall be in accordance with the laws of the land.

A Tata company, in the course of its business activities, shall respect the culture, customs and traditions of each country and region in which it operates. It shall conform to trade procedures, including licensing, documentation and other necessary formalities, as applicable.

Financial reporting and records

A Tata company shall prepare and maintain its accounts fairly and accurately and in accordance with the accounting and financial reporting standards which represent the generally accepted guidelines, principles, standards, laws and regulations of the country in which the company conducts its business affairs.

Internal accounting and audit procedures shall reflect, fairly and accurately, all of the company's business transactions and disposition of assets, and shall have internal controls to provide assurance to the company's board and shareholders that the transactions are accurate and legitimate. All required information shall be accessible to company auditors and other authorized parties and government agencies. There shall be no wilful omissions of any company transactions from the books and records, no advance-income recognition and no hidden bank account and funds.

Any wilful, material misrepresentation of and/or misinformation on the financial accounts and reports shall be regarded as a violation of the Code, apart from inviting appropriate civil or criminal action under the relevant laws. No employee shall make, authorize, abet or collude in an improper payment, unlawful commission or bribing.

Competition

A Tata company shall fully support the development and operation of competitive open markets and shall promote the liberalization of trade and investment in each country and market in which it operates. Specifically, no Tata company or employee shall engage in restrictive trade practices, abuse of market dominance or similar unfair trade activities.

A Tata company or employee shall market the company's products and services on their own merits and shall not make unfair and misleading statements about competitors' products and services. Any collection of competitive information shall be made only in the normal course of business and shall be obtained only through legally permitted sources and means.

Equal-opportunities employer

A Tata company shall provide equal opportunities to all its employees and all qualified applicants for employment without regard to their race, caste, religion, colour, ancestry, marital status, gender, sexual orientation, age, nationality, ethnic origin or disability.

Human resource policies shall promote diversity and equality in the workplace, as well as compliance with all local labour laws, while encouraging the adoption of international best practices.

Employees of a Tata company shall be treated with dignity and in accordance with the Tata policy of maintaining a work environment free of all forms of harassment, whether physical, verbal or psychological. Employee policies and practices shall be administered in a manner consistent with applicable laws and other provisions of this Code, respect for the right to privacy and the right to be heard, and that in all matters equal opportunity is provided to those eligible and decisions are based on merit.

Gifts and donations

A Tata company and its employees shall neither receive nor offer or make, directly or indirectly, any illegal payments, remuneration, gifts, donations or comparable benefits that are intended, or perceived, to obtain uncompetitive favours for the conduct of its business. The company shall cooperate with governmental authorities in efforts to eliminate all forms of bribery, fraud and corruption.

However, a Tata company and its employees may, with full disclosure, accept and offer nominal gifts, provided such gifts are customarily given and/or are of a commemorative nature. Each company shall have a policy to clarify its rules and regulations on gifts and entertainment, to be used for the guidance of its employees.

Government agencies

A Tata company and its employees shall not, unless mandated under applicable laws, offer or give any company funds or property as donation to any government agency or its representative, directly or through intermediaries, in order to obtain any favourable performance of official duties. A Tata company shall comply with government procurement regulations and shall be transparent in all its dealings with government agencies.

Political non-alignment

A Tata company shall be committed to and support the constitution and governance systems of the country in which it operates.

A Tata company shall not support any specific political party or candidate for political office. The company's conduct shall preclude any activity that could be interpreted as mutual dependence/favour with any political body or person, and shall not offer or give any company funds or property as donations to any political party, candidate or campaign.

Health, safety and environment

A Tata company shall strive to provide a safe, healthy, clean and ergonomic working environment for its people. It shall prevent the wasteful use of natural resources and be committed to improving the environment, particularly with regard to the emission of greenhouse gases, and shall endeavour to offset the effect of climate change in all spheres of its activities.

A Tata company, in the process of production and sale of its products and services, shall strive for economic, social and environmental sustainability.

Quality of products and services

A Tata company shall be committed to supply goods and services of world-class quality standards, backed by after-sales services consistent with the requirements of its customers, while striving for their total satisfaction. The quality standards of the company's goods and services shall meet applicable national and international standards.

A Tata company shall display adequate health and safety labels, caveats and other necessary information on its product packaging.

Corporate citizenship

A Tata company shall be committed to good corporate citizenship not only in the compliance of all relevant laws and regulations but also by actively assisting in the improvement of quality of life of the people in the communities in which it operates. The company shall encourage volunteering by its employees and collaboration with community groups.

Tata companies are also encouraged to develop systematic processes and conduct management reviews, as stated in the Tata 'corporate sustainability protocol', from time to time so as to set strategic direction for social development activity.

The company shall not treat these activities as optional, but should strive to incorporate them as an integral part of its business plan.

Cooperation of Tata companies

A Tata company shall cooperate with other Tata companies including applicable joint ventures, by sharing knowledge and physical, human and management resources, and by making efforts to resolve disputes amicably, as long as this does not adversely affect its business interests and shareholder value.

In the procurement of products and services, a Tata company shall give preference to other Tata companies, as long as they can provide these on competitive terms relative to third parties.

Public representation of the company and the Group

The Tata Group honours the information requirements of the public and its stakeholders. In all its public appearances, with respect to disclosing company and business information to public constituencies such as the media, the financial community, employees, shareholders, agents, franchisees, dealers, distributors and importers, a Tata company or the Tata Group shall be represented only by specifically authorized directors and employees. It shall be the sole responsibility of these authorized representatives to disclose information about the company or the Group.

Third-party representation

Parties which have business dealings with the Tata Group but are not members of the Group, such as consultants, agents, sales representatives, distributors, channel partners, contractors and suppliers, shall not be authorized to represent a Tata company without the written permission of the Tata company, and/or if their business conduct and ethics are known to be inconsistent with the Code.

Third parties and their employees are expected to abide by the Code in their interaction with, and on behalf of, a Tata company. Tata companies are encouraged to sign a nondisclosure agreement with third parties to support confidentiality of information.

Use of the Tata brand

The use of the Tata name and trademark shall be governed by manuals, codes and agreements to be issued by Tata Sons. The use of the Tata brand is defined in and regulated by the Tata Brand Equity and Business Promotion agreement. No third party or joint venture shall use the Tata brand to further its interests without specific authorization.

Group policies

A Tata company shall recommend to its board of directors the adoption of policies and guidelines periodically formulated by Tata Sons.

Shareholders

A Tata company shall be committed to enhancing shareholder value and complying with all regulations and laws that govern shareholder rights. The board of directors of a Tata company shall duly and fairly inform its shareholders about all relevant aspects of the company's business, and disclose such information in accordance with relevant regulations and agreements.

Ethical conduct

Every employee of a Tata company, including full-time directors and the chief executive, shall exhibit culturally appropriate deportment in the countries they operate in, and deal on behalf of the company with professionalism, honesty and integrity, while conforming to high moral and ethical standards. Such conduct shall be fair and transparent and be perceived to be so by third parties.

Every employee of a Tata company shall preserve the human rights of every individual and the community, and shall strive to honour commitments.

Every employee shall be responsible for the implementation of and compliance with the Code in his/ her environment. Failure to adhere to the Code could attract severe consequences, including termination of employment.

Regulatory compliance

Employees of a Tata company, in their business conduct, shall comply with all applicable laws and regulations, in letter and spirit, in all the territories in which they operate. If the ethical and professional standards of applicable laws and regulations are below that of the Code, then the standards of the Code shall prevail.

Directors of a Tata company shall comply with applicable laws and regulations of all the relevant regulatory and other authorities. As good governance practice they shall safeguard the confidentiality of all information received by them by virtue of their position.

Concurrent employment

Consistent with applicable laws, an employee of a Tata company shall not, without the requisite, officially written approval of the company, accept employment or a position of responsibility (such as a consultant or a director) with any other company, nor provide freelance services to anyone, with or without remuneration. In the case of a full-time director or the chief executive, such approval must be obtained from the board of directors of the company.

Conflict of interest

An employee or director of a Tata company shall always act in the interest of the company, and ensure that any business or personal association which he/she may have does not involve a conflict of interest with the operations of the company and his/her role therein.

An employee, including the executive director (other than independent director) of a Tata company, shall not accept a position of responsibility in any other non-Tata company or not-for-profit organization without specific sanction.

The above shall not apply to (whether for remuneration or otherwise):

- Nominations to the boards of Tata companies, joint ventures or associate companies.
- Memberships/positions of responsibility in educational/professional bodies, wherein such association will benefit the employee/Tata company.

- Nominations/memberships in government committees/bodies or organizations.
- Exceptional circumstances, as determined by the competent authority.

Competent authority, in the case of all employees, shall be the chief executive, who in turn shall report such exceptional cases to the board of directors on a quarterly basis. In case of the chief executive and executive directors, the Group Corporate Centre shall be the competent authority.

An employee or a director of a Tata company shall not engage in any business, relationship or activity which might conflict with the interest of his/her company or the Tata Group. A conflict of interest, actual or potential, may arise where, directly or indirectly:

- An employee of a Tata company engages in a business, relationship or activity with anyone who is party to a transaction with his/her company.
- An employee is in a position to derive an improper benefit, personally or to any of his/her relatives, by making or influencing decisions relating to any transaction.

- An independent judgement of the company's or Group's best interest cannot be exercised.

The main areas of such actual or potential conflicts of interest shall include the following:

- An employee or a full-time director of a Tata company conducting business on behalf of his/her company or being in a position to influence a decision with regard to his/her company's business with a supplier or customer where his/her relative is a principal officer or representative, resulting in a benefit to him/her or his/her relative.
- Award of benefits such as increase in salary or other remuneration, posting, promotion or recruitment of a relative of an employee of a Tata company, where such an individual is in a position to influence decisions with regard to such benefits.
- The interest of the company or the Group can be compromised or defeated.

Notwithstanding such or any other instance of conflict of interest that exist due to historical reasons, adequate and full disclosure by interested employees shall be made to the company's management. It is also incumbent upon every employee to make a full disclosure of any interest which the employee or the employee's immediate family, including parents, spouse and children, may have in a family business or a company or firm that is a competitor, supplier, customer or distributor of or has other business dealings with his/her company.

Upon a decision being taken in the matter, the employee concerned shall be required to take necessary action, as advised, to resolve/avoid the conflict.

If an employee fails to make the required disclosure and the management of its own accord becomes aware of an instance of conflict of interest that ought to have been disclosed by the employee, the management shall take a serious view of the matter and consider suitable disciplinary action against the employee.

Securities transactions and confidential information

An employee of a Tata company and his/her immediate family shall not derive any benefit or counsel, or assist others to derive any benefit, from access to and possession of information about the company or Group or its clients or suppliers that is not in the public domain and, thus, constitutes unpublished, price-sensitive insider information.

An employee of a Tata company shall not use or proliferate information that is not available to the investing public, and which therefore constitutes insider information, for making or giving advice on investment decisions about the securities of the respective Tata company, Group, client or supplier on which such insider information has been obtained.

Such insider information might include (without limitation) the following:

- Acquisition and divestiture of businesses or business units.
- Financial information such as profits, earnings and dividends.
- Announcement of new product introductions or developments.
- Asset revaluations.
- Investment decisions/plans.

- Restructuring plans.
- Major supply and delivery agreements.
- Raising of finances.

An employee of a Tata company shall also respect and observe the confidentiality of information pertaining to other companies, their patents, intellectual property rights, trademarks and inventions; and strictly observe a practice of non-disclosure.

Protecting company assets

The assets of a Tata company shall not be misused; they shall be employed primarily and judiciously for the purpose of conducting the business for which they are duly authorized. These include tangible assets such as equipment and machinery, systems, facilities, materials and resources, as well as intangible assets such as information technology and systems, proprietary information, intellectual property, and relationships with customers and suppliers.

Citizenship

The involvement of a Tata employee in civic or public affairs shall be with express approval from the chief executive of his/her company, subject to this involvement having no adverse impact on the business affairs of the company or the Tata Group.

Integrity of data furnished

Every employee of a Tata company shall ensure, at all times, the integrity of data or information furnished by him/her to the company. He/she shall be entirely responsible in ensuring that the confidentiality of all data is retained and in no circumstance transferred to any outside person/party in the course of normal operations without express guidelines from, or the approval of the management.

Reporting concerns

Every employee of a Tata company shall promptly report to the management, and/or third-party ethics helpline, when she/he becomes aware of any actual or possible violation of the Code or an event of misconduct, act of misdemeanour or act not in the company's interest. Such reporting shall be made available to suppliers and partners, too.

Any Tata employee can choose to make a protected disclosure under the whistleblower policy of the company, providing for reporting to the chairperson of the audit committee or the board of directors or specified authority. Such a protected disclosure shall be forwarded, when there is reasonable evidence to conclude that a violation is possible or has taken place, with a covering letter, which shall bear the identity of the whistleblower.

The company shall ensure protection to the whistleblower and any attempts to intimidate him/her would be treated as a violation of the Code.

Note:

The TCoC does not provide a full, comprehensive and complete explanation of all the rules that employees are bound to follow. Employees have a continuing obligation to familiarize themselves with all applicable laws, company policies, procedures and work rules.

All JVs could adopt TCoC or a joint code of conduct incorporating all elements of the TCoC.

This version of the TCoC supersedes all earlier versions and associated documents and stands effective from October 1, 2013.

LETTER FROM JAMSETJI TATA TO LORD REAY

Jasmetji outlines to Lord Reay, Governor of Bombay, his vision for a new affordable educational institution outside of the then class-based system.

Bombay, 27th November, 1896

Dear Lord Reay,

I must apologise at the outset for troubling you at some length on a subject which is occupying my thoughts. My excuse must be that the topic is one in which you have manifested great interest to the extent of thinking out a comprehensive scheme in detail. I am labouring only to translate into action the wise reflections expressed in the chancellor's address at the Convocation for the year 1889/90.

Being blessed by the Mercy of Providence with more than a fair share of the world's goods, and persuaded that I owe much of my success in life to an unusual combination of favouring circumstances, I have felt incumbent on myself to help to provide a continuous sphere of such circumstances for my less fortunate countrymen.

It is not adequately realized how much the efficiency of general education must depend in the last result on the efficiency of the Highest University Education. The improvement of university education is the key of all educational improvement; for no important innovation in lower tuition can be entrusted to illiberally trained minds.

Three things appear to be desiderated thereof: a comprehensive and practical scheme of university reform based on more elevated conceptions of the functions of a university; a constitution of the governing body of the University, such, that the continuity of reforming activity on fixed lines may be ensured by being attached to the permanent public opinion of the permanent residents of the country; and lastly, ample funds to execute all these ideas on an adequate scale.

The framework of the first desideratum exists ready to hand in your Lordship's chancellorial address and I shall be prepared to engage experts in whose choice I should require your help to work the Scheme out, into practical details.

Several alternative procedures suggest themselves at this stage:

(1) a new University to be formed to carry out these ideas,

(2) the present Bombay University to be converted into a teaching University, much on the same lines as are proposed for its prototype—the London University, with a changed constitution and ample scope for the introduction of the higher conceptions of University teaching,

(3) the taking over of the Elphinstone and Grant Colleges by a duly constituted Board such as govern

the Sindh or the Gujrat College, to whom must, of course, be assigned the present Government expenditure on whose institution, provided, the Corporation and private enterprise add a considerably higher sum and with these funds work out reforms, on a scale compatible with affiliation to the existing University, or

(4) starting a new College on these principles.

It may also be desirable to continue with any of these, the plan of a National University for India, conferring diplomas on candidates who pass this University's examination, after graduating at one of the local Universities. The speciality and capacity for research in the local Universities may thus be stimulated as the Ferguson Scholarships have stimulated them in Scotland. The second want—the provision of an improved constitution for the proposed university or college—may be suitably studied along with the first by the experts referred to.

Your Lordship probably thinks that the provision of funds is the crux of the problem. I am aware that the quality of the Professorate itself has to be enlarged; that to provide resource for research, they have to be furnished a body of assistants, lecturers and tutors; that laboratories, museums, workshops, antiquities have all to be supplied; and all mean vast sums of money.

No single man's resources in India can cope with all these wants, though individuals may do much. No individual has therefore a right to attach conditions to his gifts, which might impede other benefactors. I am convinced, that if a firm lead is given, such benefactors will stream in upon the new or recognised University, if purely and sincerely managed as a National University. It is my firm belief, that Corporation, the Native Chiefs, Sirdars, and Native gentry will generally see their way to bountifully help such an institution.

I propose to give such a lead by making a Trust Settlement of property annually yielding between Rupees Eighty thousand and a lac for this purpose; subject, however, to certain stipulations. I want no titles for myself; nor do I wish my name attached to anything.

The National movement ought to bear a National name; and every separate benefactor might be at ease, as far as I am concerned, that his endowment won't bear a name subsidiary to any. I have executed a

Trust Settlement in favour of my two sons and their descendants (a copy of which I will send to your Lordship later on) and I wish to combine this Settlement with the one I propose for the contemplated University.

The above reasons, combined with a desire to make a permanent Settlement for my family, prompts me to trouble your Lordship to aid and advise me in the initiation of this work. If you but pronounce an opinion as to the feasibility of the proposed Scheme, I will, as early as possible send over a young friend of mine, lately Vice Principal of the Sind College, Kurrachee, who has studied the question of a teaching National University for India.

In consultation with you, and with your advice, he would first have a comprehensive Scheme prepared by a competent Parliamentary draftsman, whom your Lordship may recommend. On this draft being sent over here and approved, I would beg of your Lordship, with your vast experience and reputation as an Educationist and your influence in such matters with the Government and Public at home, to have it passed in the Legislature of course, with the previous approval and sanction of the Governments in India.

The funds that I propose to place at the disposal of the Governing body are not so very large for the purpose, but we all hope to augment them considerably, by appealing, as I have hinted above, to our patriotic nobility, gentry and the professional and trading classes, with fair prospects of a very favourable response.

Yours etc.

Sd Jamsetji N Tata

A TATA TIMELINE

1857   The Sepoy Mutiny or the First War of Independence in India; India comes under direct British rule, with power transferring from the East India Company, in 1858, following the mutiny.

1868   Jamsetji Nusserwanji Tata starts a private trading firm, laying the foundation of the Tata Group.

1874   The Central India Spinning, Weaving and Manufacturing Company is set up, marking the Group's entry into textiles and its first large-scale industrial venture.

1902   The Indian Hotels Company is incorporated to set up the Taj Mahal Palace Hotel, India's first luxury hotel, which opens in Bombay in 1903.

1904   Sir Dorabji Tata takes over as chairman of the
        Tata Group of companies after his father Jamsetji's
        passing.

1907   The Tata Iron and Steel Company (now Tata Steel)
        is established to set up India's first iron and steel
        plant in Jamshedpur; the plant starts production in
        1912.

1910   The first of the three Tata Electric Companies, the
        Tata Hydro-Electric Power Supply Company, is
        set up. The three companies became Tata Power
        in 2000.

1911   The Indian Institute of Science is established
        in Bangalore to serve as a centre for advanced
        learning.

1912   Tata Steel introduces eight-hour working days, well
        before such a system was implemented by law in
        much of the West.

1917   The Tatas enter the consumer goods industry with
        the Tata Oil Mills Company being established
        to make soaps, detergents and cooking oils. The
        company was sold to Hindustan Lever (now
        Unilever) in the early 1990s.

1932   Sir Nowroji Saklawata, the son of Jamsetji's sister, becomes the third chairman of the Tata Group after the death of his cousin Sir Dorabji Tata.

Tata Airlines, a division of Tata Sons, is established, opening up the aviation sector in India. It would become Air-India, which was nationalized in 1953.

1938   Following the death of Sir Nowroji Saklawata, Jamsetji Tata's cousin's son, Jehangir Ratanji Dadabhoy Tata, takes the helm as the fourth chairman of the group.

1939–45   World War II.

1939   Tata Chemicals, now the largest producer of soda ash in the country, is established.

1944   The 'Bombay Plan', a plan for the economic development of India, formulated by leading industrialists, is published; J.R.D. Tata is one of the signatories.

1945   The Tata Engineering and Locomotive Company (now known as Tata Motors) is established to manufacture locomotive and engineering products.

Tata Industries is created for the promotion and development of hi-tech industries.

1947 India becomes independent.

1950 The Constitution of independent India declares it to be a secular socialist republic.

1952 Jawaharlal Nehru, India's first prime minister, requests the group to manufacture cosmetics in India, leading to the setting up of Lakmé. The company was sold to Hindustan Lever (now Unilever) in 1997.

1954 India's major marketing, engineering and manufacturing organization Voltas is established.

1962 Tata Finlay (later renamed Tata Tea and then Tata Global Beverages), one of the largest tea producers in the world, is established.

Tata Exports is established; today, the company, renamed Tata International, is one of the leading export houses in India.

1968 TCS, India's first software services company, is established.

1971   Tata Precision Industries, the first Tata company in Singapore, is founded to design and manufacture precision engineering products.

1975– Emergency is imposed in India by Indira Gandhi's
77   government, curtailing individual freedom. The Congress is voted out of power after the Emergency is lifted in 1977.

1984   After her return to power (in 1980), Prime Minister Indira Gandhi is assassinated; her son Rajiv Gandhi becomes prime minister.

The first 500 MW thermal power unit at the Trombay station of the Tata Electric Companies is commissioned.

1991   Rajiv Gandhi, now out of power, is assassinated.

Economic liberalization seen in India; the economy is opened up to global players.

Following the retirement of J.R.D. Tata, Ratan Tata becomes the fifth chairman of the group.

1995   Tata Quality Management Services institutes the JRD QV Award, modelled on the Malcolm Baldrige

National Quality Award of the United States, laying the foundation of the Tata Business Excellence Model.

1996   Tata Teleservices is established to spearhead the group's foray into the telecom sector.

1998   The right-wing Bharatiya Janata Party (BJP), heading a coalition, comes to power in India.

India carries out nuclear tests and becomes a nuclear power.

Tata Indica—India's first indigenously designed and manufactured car—is launched by Tata Motors, spearheading the group's entry into the passenger-car segment

1999   The new Tata Group corporate mark and logo are launched.

2000   India hits the 1-billion population mark.

Tata Tea acquires the Tetley Group, UK. This is the first major acquisition of an international brand by an Indian business group.

2001   Tata AIG—a joint venture between the Tata Group and the American International Group Inc. (AIG)— marks Tata's re-entry into insurance.

2002   Tata Sons acquires a controlling stake in VSNL (now known as Tata Communications), India's leading international telecommunications service provider.

2003   TCS becomes the first Indian software company to cross $1 billion in revenues.

Tata Teleservices launches the Tata Indicom (now Tata Docomo) mobile service.

2004   The Congress returns to power, heading a coalition; Manmohan Singh, the architect of economic liberalization, becomes prime minister.

Tata Motors is listed on the world's largest bourse, the New York Stock Exchange, the second group company to do so after VSNL (now known as Tata Communications).

TCS goes public in the largest private sector IPO in the Indian market, raising nearly $1.2 billion.

Indian Hotels unveils indiOne (now known as Ginger Hotels), a first-of-its-kind chain of smart, basic hotels.

2005   Tata Motors creates a new mini-truck segment in India with the launch of Tata Ace.

Trent acquires strategic interest in the Landmark chain of bookstores.

2006   India and the United States sign a nuclear agreement.

The Tata Sky satellite television service is launched across the country.

Infiniti Retail launches Croma, India's first national chain of multi-brand outlets for consumer electronics and durable products.

2007   Tata Steel acquires the Anglo-Dutch company Corus (now known as Tata Steel Europe), making it the world's fifth-largest steel producer.

Computational Research Laboratories, a division of Tata Sons, develops Eka, one of the fastest supercomputers in the world and the fastest in Asia.

Tata Capital is established as a new Tata company in the financial sector.

2008   Tata Motors unveils Tata Nano, the People's Car; it also acquires the Jaguar and Land Rover brands from the Ford Motor Company.

2009   Tata Chemicals launches Tata Swach—the world's most cost-effective water purifier.

Tata Housing makes waves with the launch of its low-cost housing in Mumbai.

2010   Advinus Therapeutics announces the discovery of a novel molecule—GKM-001—for the treatment of Type II diabetes.

Tata Tea announces a joint venture with PepsiCo, for health drinks.

2011   The Tata brand soars into the top 50 club of global brands.

Tata Medical Centre, a comprehensive cancer care and treatment facility, is inaugurated.

Tata BP Solar becomes a wholly-owned Tata company (now known as Tata Power Solar Systems).

2012   Following the retirement of Ratan Tata, Cyrus Mistry becomes the sixth chairman of the group.

Tata Global Beverages and Starbucks form joint venture to open Starbucks cafes across India.

Tata Communications completes the world's first wholly-owned cable network ring around the world.

India's first iodine-plus-iron-fortified salt is launched by Tata Chemicals.

2013   Tata Power synchronizes its fifth 800 MW unit and makes its first ultra mega power project (UMPP) of 4000 MW at Mundra fully operational.

Tata Sons announces formation of the Group Executive Council.

Tata Sons and Singapore Airlines collaborate to establish a new airline in India.

2014   The BJP returns to power with a majority in Parliament as a single party; Narendra Modi becomes prime minister.

BIBLIOGRAPHY

Alhanati, Joao, 'Follow Your Passions and Success Will Follow', Investopedia.com, 20 July 2012; available online at: http://www.investopedia.com/articles/pf/12/passion-success.asp.

Chakravorty, Jui, 'Analysis: Tradition, sprawl confront next Tata Group Leader', Reuters, 27 May 2011; available online at: http://uk.reuters.com/article/2011/05/27/us-tata-succession-idUKTRE74Q0IV20110527.

CNN Travel, 'Mumbai without Parsis: A selfish and sick city'; available online at: http://travel.cnn.com/mumbai/life/what-would-mumbai-be-without-its-parsis-032539.

Corrente, Will, 'The Importance of Building Your

Business on Your Passion', Entrepreneur Week, 16 March 2012; available online at: http://www. entrepreneurweek.net/articles/the-importance-of-building-your-business-on-your-passion.

Dadrawala, Noshir, 'The Parsees, Their History, Religion and Contribution To Indian Society'; available online at: http://www.zawa.asn.au/history2.shtml.

Dadrawala, Noshir, 'Parsi Thy Name is Charity'; available online at: http://zoroastrians.net/2011/08/17/ parsi-charity-and-philanthropy.

The Economist, 'From Pupil to Master', 1 December 2012; available online at: http://www.economist.com/ news/21567390-ratan-tatas-successor-cyrus-mistry-has-some-dirty-work-do-pupil-master.

Ja, Sneha, 'TCS' Road to the Top', CEO Interview, CIO; available online at: http://www.cio.in/ceo-interviews/ tcs-road-top.

Gale Encyclopedia of Biography: Jamsetji Nusserwanji Tata.

Harris, Frank, *Jamsetji Nusserwanji Tata—A Chronicle of His Life*, Blackie and Son Ltd, 1958.

Kalbag, Chaitanya and Goutam Das, 'TCS CEO Chandrasekaran on changing nature of his business, leadership, and people plans', *BusinessToday*, 23 October 2013; available online at: http://businesstoday. intoday.in/storyprint/199788#.

Lala, R.M., *The Creation of Wealth: The Tatas from the 19th to the 21st Century*, Penguin Books India: New Delhi, 2004.

Majumdar Boria and Mehta Nalin, *Olympics: The India Story*. Chapter: '100 Yards Round A Bend' To Antwerp: Peasants On The Athletics Track'.

Merchant, Nilofer, 'Steve Jobs's Legacy: Design Your Own Life', HBR blog, 6 October 2011; available online at: http://blogs.hbr.org/2011/10/steve-jobs-legacy-design-your.

Murthy, N.R. Narayana, 'Let There be more Ratans so that India Can Shine Like a Diamond', *The Economic*

Times, 8 April 2013; available online at: http://articles.economictimes.indiatimes.com/2013-04-08/news/38373917_1_ratan-sudha-hubli.

Nadkarni, Anant and Oana Branzei, 'The Tata Way: Evolving and executing sustainable business strategies', *Ivey Business Journal*, April 2008; available online at: http://iveybusinessjournal.com/topics/strategy/the-tata-way-evolving-and-executing-sustainable-business-strategies.

Noronha, Christabelle, *Lasting Legacies*, Tata Commemorative edition, 2004.

Olesia, Wekesa et al, 'Role of Servant Leadership on Organizational Commitment', *International Journal of Humanities and Social Science*, 2013; available online at: http://www.ijhssnet.com/journals/Vol_3_No_13_July_2013/11.pdf

Pecorino, Philip, Philosophy of Religion class, Queensborough Community College, 2001; available online at: http://www.qcc.cuny.edu/socialsciences/

ppecorino/phil_of_religion_text/CHAPTER_2_
RELIGIONS/Zoroastrianism.htm.

Rai, Saritha, 'India's TCS Becomes the World's Second
Most Valuable IT Services Firm', *Forbes*, 13 September
2013; available online at: http://www.forbes.com/
sites/saritharai/2013/09/13/indias-tcs-is-second-most-
valuable-it-services-firm-globally/.

Sangghvi, Malavika, 'Saying Sorry in Style', Mid-Day.
com, August 2013; available online at: http://www.
mid-day.com/columnists/2013/aug/190813-parsi-new-
year-jehangir-sabavala-jrd-tata.htm.

Shinde, Shivani, 'What Makes TCS tick?', *Business
Standard*, 1 May 2013; available online at: http://www.
business-standard.com/article/companies/what-makes-
tcs-tick-113050100844_1.html.

Spence, Rick, 'The Importance of Business Passion—
At any age', *Business Financial Post*, 9 November
2013; available online at: http://business.financialpost.
com/2013/09/11/the-importance-of-business-passion-
at-any-age.

Stibel, Jeff, 'Would You Rather be Revolutionary or Evolutionary?', HBR Blog Network, 22 June 2011; available online at: http://blogs.hbr.org/2011/06/would-you-rather-be-revolution/.

Tata Group website: http://www.tata.co.in/default

Witzel, Morgan, *TATA: The Evolution of a Corporate Brand*, Penguin: New Delhi, 2010.

ACKNOWLEDGEMENTS

I decided to write this book after becoming fascinated with the story behind the amazing company named Tata and its unique structure. It has been a voyage of discovery, and one in which I became more enchanted at every step. Although this book was written independently of Tata, I would like to thank all those in the company who have helped and encouraged me, not least Rajendra Prasad Narla and the staff of the Tata Archives, who have been a fountain of knowledge and generosity.

And, finally, I would like to thank my wife and children, who are my inspiration.

INDEX

NOTES ON THE AUTHOR
AND THE ILLUSTRATOR

About the Author

Peter Casey is founder and executive chairman of Claddagh Resources, a global recruitment and search business that places high-level executives with many of the world's Fortune 500 companies. Having established successful business interests in Australia and Ireland, Peter set up Claddagh Resources in Atlanta, Georgia in 1995. Claddagh currently operates on four continents.

Peter was named by *Irish America* magazine as one of the leading Irish-American businessmen for 2007. He has had a wide portfolio of business interests, including commercial, residential and agricultural property in Ireland. His approach to business is simple—he likes to invest in people. Peter is also an accomplished writer and a political and business commentator, with articles published regularly in Ireland and the United States. He is best known, perhaps, as an investor on the Irish television programme *Dragons' Den*, in which he is one of the Dragons. He tweets with the handle @TheDragonPeter. You can find out more about his work at www.petercasey.ie.

Peter lives in Atlanta with his wife, Helen, and their five children, and divides his time between there and his family home in Derry. Outside work he enjoys playing golf badly!

About the Illustrator

Mike Luckovich is a two-time Pulitzer Prize-winning editorial cartoonist who has worked for *The Atlanta Journal-Constitution* since 1989. He won the Reuben, the National Cartoonists Society's top award for cartoonist of the year, in 2005.